Welcome to The Cornish Garden in its ne[w format]

As your new editor I have had the rare opportunity of bei[ng able] to design the Society's Journal to maintain its position as [the] premier garden society Journal. Roger Trenoweth had al[ready set the standard] by his contributions over the last 18 years culminating in [his excellent 50th] anniversary compilation which will be of particular interest to those who do not have a full set of back copies.

It is almost inevitable with any change that there will be some who would have preferred to keep things as they were, but I would like to imagine that Brigadier A. W. G. Wildey, who edited the first seven issues, would be impressed by the way that the Journal has developed since those early days and that the general membership would feel dispirited if the current issue still had a flavour of 1957, the year that Sputnik was launched and Harold Macmillan became Prime Minister.

As a result of the changes, it is now possible to have coloured photos on all pages and in a format which encourages the "coffee table" approach.

I have very much enjoyed producing the Journal and it has been a privilege to receive such positive responses from those whom I have asked for articles. As you will see, they have responded with great generosity by donating erudite pieces and they have either provided their own illustrations or allowed me to take photos to add pictures to their words. Indeed, this generous spirit has not been confined solely to people with an innate interest in Cornish gardens: for Eric Milner Kay's article I was able to provide a photo of an *Amanita muscaria* but, although my wife and I spent an afternoon searching the larch plantations near Pencarrow, we could not find a *Boletus elegans* to photograph, then I looked on the internet where I found a lovely example beautifully photographed by Lara Stefansdottir in Iceland. A couple of e-mails later she had very kindly sent me a high resolution copy at no cost to the Society. Anyone contemplating visiting Iceland would do well to look through her excellent range of photos at www.flickr.com/photos/lastef.

For anyone who is averse to change, I'm afraid that there is further bad news in that we also have a new logo! Such changes are always contentious, particularly as they are usually accompanied in the press by an exposé of how much some high-profile company has spent on a design agency. However, I can reassure you that, in this instance, this is definitely not the case. For many years the idea of changing the logo has been under consideration and your executive decided that the time had finally come to grasp the nettle and take action. Accordingly, they asked the Graphic Design course students at University College Falmouth to come up with some suggestions. Their work was excellent and the decision was not easily reached, however, it was felt that Krystal Fanning's design achieved all the right features and we are very grateful to her. Hopefully she will now go on to enjoy a career where she can charge unfeasibly large fees to high-profile companies. You can read her own thoughts about the contest on page 8.

Naturally I should be delighted to hear from anyone who would be interested in contributing to the 2009 Journal and, of course, from anyone who wishes to advertise with us.

Kind regards

Charles Francis
Editor

Photo Charles Francis
The Sundial Garden in the Lost Gardens of Heligan

9

24

16

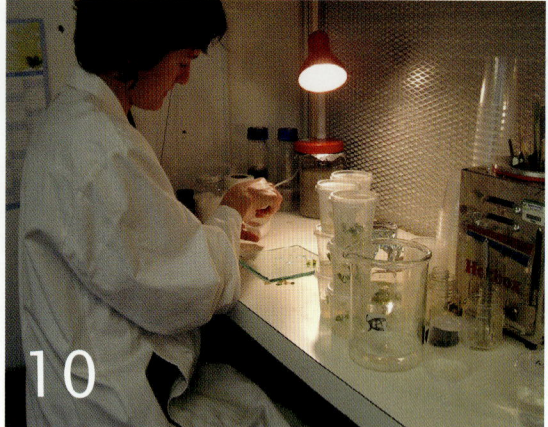
10

28

18

CONTENTS

6 Reports from the AGM
Speeches by the Chairman and President. Lecture by Penelope Hobhouse

9 New CGS logo design
Krystal Fanning's new logo design is unveiled

10 Conserving heritage plants through micropropagation
Ros Smith explains the work being done at Duchy College

16 BBC Radio Cornwall's Gardenline
Tim Hubbard talks about the gardening side of his career

18 To dig or not to dig?
That is the question posed and answered by Eric Milner Kay

24 Lanterns Garden
Heather Hall describes how she raises money for the "Precious Lives Appeal"

28 This sporting life
Bee Robson looks at how new camellia cultivars are created from sports

36 **Enys Gardens, St Gluvias**
Barry Champion visits this historic garden

42 **Becoming a botanist**
Keith Spurgin looks at some visitors to your garden in a different light

46 **Here's food for thought**
John Mann presents an entertaining diary of the Society's summer tour to the Cotswolds

55 **Boconnoc - The future**
Anthony Fortescue discusses the changing ways of timber management

66 **Garden photography**
Charles Francis provides some tips for improving your garden photography

72 **Cover story**
Cindy Clench explains how tree ferns came to Cornwall

CGS Trustees/Directors and other officers

Judith Hancock
Vice-Chairman

Elizabeth Wilton
Hon. Secretary

Giles Bingley FCA
Treasurer

Giles Clotworthy

Peter Gilmore
Events Co-ordinator

Sarah Gordon

Jenni Hilliard
Vice-President

Deborah Hinton OBE
Publicity

Nigel Holman
Vice-President

Christian Lamb

Andrew Leslie

Nutty Lim

John Mann

Brenda Salmon

Sally-Jane Coode
Show Director

Debbie Evans
Walks & Talks

Charles Francis
Journal Editor

Tessa Phipps
Schools gardening

Alison Voelcker
Lectures Organiser

Pat Ward
Membership Sec.

THE CORNISH GARDEN

THE JOURNAL OF THE CORNWALL GARDEN SOCIETY

MARCH 2008

ISSUE 51

MEMBERSHIP BENEFITS

The benefits of membership are:-

Privileged admission to the CGS Spring Show

FREE admission to lectures held monthly between October and April, at various locations county-wide, featuring national speakers as well as informative local gardeners.

The chance to exchange garden tips, ideas, knowledge and, of course plants with other members (and to see round their gardens and make new friends)

Regular visits to interesting and outstanding gardens, with special 'walks and talks'.

Garden theme holiday

The CGS Journal, newsletter, programme and information mailed to you.

For fuller information and subscription rates please contact the Membership Secretary:
Pat Ward, Poltisko, Silver Hill, Perranwell Station,
Truro TR3 7LP

or visit our website: www.cornwallgardensoc.ik.com

Edited, designed and produced by Charles Francis
Charles Francis Photography + Design
The Wagon House, Heligan Manor
St Ewe, Cornwall PL26 6EW
www.thewagonhouse.com

ISBN 978-0-9516410-1-9

Printed by Francis Antony Ltd. St Austell, Cornwall

Published by The Cornwall Garden Society, c/o The Wagon House, Heligan Manor, St Ewe, Cornwall PL26 6EW

© 2008 The Cornwall Garden Society and contributors. All rights reserved.
The contents of this Journal are fully protected by copyright and may not be reproduced without permission.
Opinions expressed by authors and services offered by advertisers are not specifically endorsed by the Society.
The Cornish Garden is made from paper from sustainable sources.

Cover photo by Charles Francis - *Dicksonia antarctica* in the Lost Gardens of Heligan

CGS Annual General Meeting and Penelope Hobhouse lecture

The Society's A.G.M. took place in the Keay Theatre at John Keay House, St Austell on 9th October 2007. We commenced with a minute's silence as a sign of respect for the late Lady Falmouth who made such an enormous contribution to the Society over so many years. The A.G.M. itself was well attended and then the remaining seats in the theatre filled quickly as Penelope Hobhouse prepared to deliver her illustrated lecture on "The Gardens of Islam: Mirrors of Paradise". As usual, her talk was eloquent and filled with fascinating facts about her subject, for example, the pattern on some Persian rugs is based around the long thin rectangular pool which forms such a feature of Islamic garden design. One of her photos, from an aeroplane, showed the extraordinary isolation of one these gardens in the desert, emphasising the total reliance on the irrigation system.

Penelope Hobhouse
Photo Charles Francis

Report by the Society's Chairman Bryan Coode:

You have all received the AGM report and will have read the summary of all the Society's activities. There is therefore no point in my repeating it, particularly when we have the important and I am sure fascinating lecture by Penelope Hobhouse starting soon.

In summary, the CGS has continued its steady growth of membership and financial stability. The Executive and Trustees have achieved this by adopting a business-like approach and have tried to achieve a "virtuous spiral" of improvements and benefits without increasing subscriptions and to give back increasing value to members, such as improved quality newsletters, an easier to follow new events programme booklet (both organised by Pat Ward), and possibly a changed Journal next year by Charles Francis and of course the free book of Journal articles produced by Roger Trenoweth - A Triumph!

This "virtuous spiral" has been achieved by:
- Control of costs
- Efficiency of organisation
- Growth

We try hard on these three areas.

The AGM is always a good opportunity to thank publicly the Executive members who really do contribute an enormous amount of their time to making everything happen. Fortunately the team has largely stayed together, so it is not necessary to dwell on this but, could I please summarise the key players: Alice Boyd as our President, Giles Bingley as Treasurer, Elizabeth Wilton as Secretary, Judith Hancock as Deputy Chairman and Deborah Hinton for Publicity. Roger Trenoweth who has now handed the Journal over to Charles Francis, Tessa Phillips for Gardening in Schools and of course all the non-executive trustees who are listed in the report. They all represent the lower profile team that the members do not often see but carry out the vital roles very conscientiously.

In contrast, Sally-Jane's role over the Show is high profile, as is Pat Ward's with membership, Peter Gilmore's and Judy Lodge's with outings, Sarah Gordon's and now Debbie Evans with Walks and Talks, and Nutty Lim who has now handed over to Alison Voelcker to run our high profile Lecture programme.

I personally owe them a great debt of gratitude for their support and, ladies and gentlemen, venture to suggest that you may feel the same.

A farewell is due to Charlotte Petherwick who has been a mainstay of our Society for many years as member, Council Member, Chairman and President as she has decided to stand down from the Board of Trustees. Her wise and calm voice has always been sound and perceptive, to which she has always added many qualities including a great charm and sense of humour. We have asked her to become an Honorary Vice President.

A special mention to Roger Trenoweth - He has run the Journal for 18 years with great dedication and skill, producing an excellent erudite, prestigious, high quality Journal which has been enjoyed tremendously by members. We are most grateful to Roger for everything he has done so selflessly.

Pat tells me our membership has now reached 1525, up from 1433 in the report. If in the future any members have any suggestions, thoughts or concerns, do please contact any members of the Executive or Trustees at any time to share them. All our contact details are on the newsletter.

Finally may I please thank you, the members, for supporting the events and for being so cheerful, knowledgeable and enthusiastic. it is a privilege for me to be Chairman of your Society.

Report by the President, Viscountess Boyd JP. DL.

Good evening ladies and gentlemen - it gives me great pleasure to welcome so many of you to our AGM. The Cornwall Garden Society was formed in 1957 from the old Cornwall Daffodil and Spring Flower Society which started in 1897, so a Happy Birthday to us! It's been a great honour to be President during the last year - though this is not an arduous role owing to the tremendous work done by our Chairman - Bryan Coode and I should like to thank him very much indeed for the huge commitment he has made to the Society. Thank you Bryan.

The fortunes of the Society continue to thrive due to the incredible amount of time and effort given by both the Executive members of the committee and the countless volunteers who help in a thousand different ways - many of whom are here tonight - all because we love gardening and plants. Thank you all.

Our most well known event is the Spring Flower Show at Boconnoc. The others are lectures during the autumn and winter months and walks and talks during the spring and summer. All of these take a formidable amount of organisation by people who have probably got completely full lives already but are tremendously enjoyed by the participants. To all who help to organise these events I would like to give my grateful thanks.

To return to the Spring Flower Show which, this year, made an increased profit. A big thank you to everyone who exhibited in the competitive classes which were once again of a very high standard and are one of the most popular parts of the Show. I know what a lot of effort goes into bringing flowers for exhibition but it is enormously appreciated, so please continue to do so and indeed encourage other people and show them how to do it.

The Chairman has paid tribute to Sally-Jane Coode, the Show Director, in his report but I would like to add my special thanks - it's easier for me as I'm not married to her - and I do think she should be recognised as the person who has contributed most to the Society's present healthy financial position. She directs the Show in her extraordinarily calm way, nothing seems to phase her and potential crises seem to melt away. Sally-Jane thank you very much.

The operation of the Society is a team effort but I must mention Pat Ward. She is called the Membership Secretary but although that is a most important job and she does it perfectly, it gives a very over-simplified impression of what she does. She knows every aspect of how the Society works and at some time or other has done, or does, nearly every job. She and Mary Hutt make a formidable team and we are very grateful to them.

Now that is enough from me, so let's get on with the meeting.

Spring Flower Show at Boconnoc 2007

The Society was fortunate to have perfect weather for the Spring Flower Show, in a year which had some of the wettest months since records began in the 1730s.

The trade stands contained items of interest for all gardeners and the competitive classes were well contested with the results as shown on page 8.

Photos Charles Francis

Visit to Chyverton

Following the successful CGS Spring Flower Show at Boconnoc in 2007, Nigel Holman kindly invited all show helpers to visit his garden at Chyverton for a guided tour followed by tea. Although the weather was damp, this did not detract from our visit as we explored the grounds.

Photo Charles Francis

PRESENTATION OF AWARDS

CGS SPRING FLOWER SHOW 2007

Section A – TREES AND SHRUBS
1. **The Rosemary Cobbald-Sawle Cup** ....TREBAH GARDENS
    Best Exhibit in Class 1 Section A
2. **The Louis Reid Cup** ....THE EDEN PROJECT
    Most Points Class 2-7 Section A
3. **The Moira Reid Memorial Trophy** ....T CHRISTOPHERS(Hayle)
    Best Exhibit of variegated foliage Section A

Section B – MAGNOLIAS
4. **The George Johnstone Perpetual Trophy** CAERHAYS CASTLE GARDENS
    Most points Magnolia classes Section B
5. **The Treve Holman Memorial Cup** ....CAERHAYS CASTLE GARDENS
    Best Exhibit in Section B

Section C – CAMELLIAS
6. **The Norman Colville Bowl** ....DUCHY OF CORNWALL NURSERIES
    Best Exhibit in Class 13 (12 diff blooms)
7. **The Viscountess Boyd of Merton Cup** ....MRS C PETHERICK (St Austell)
    Best Exhibit in Class 35
8. **The Camellia Cup** ....MOUNT EDGCUMBE
    Most points in Section C
9. **The Coode Camellia Cup** ....MRS J COOK (Falmouth)
    Most points Section C under 1/2 acre

Section D – RHODODENDRONS
10. **The Mrs Charles Williams Rhododendron Cup**..TREWITHEN GARDENS
    Most points in Section D
11. **The E J P Magor Memorial Cup** ....TREWITHEN GARDENS
    Best Vase or Exhibit 39-58,62 & 63
12. **Abiss Memorial Trophy** (Best Section A,B,C,D)
    Vase or growing plant..................CAERHAYS CASTLE GARDENS

Section E – DAFFODILS
13. **The John Levitt Memorial Cup** ....R G SLEEMAN (Truro)
    Most points single bloom
    69,71,73,75,77,79,81,83,85,87,89,91,93,95.
14. **The Charles Le Grice Cup** ....R G SLEEMAN (Truro)
    Most points 3 stem
    68,70,72,74,76,78,80,82,84,86,88,90,92,94.
15. **The Edward Pedlar Cup** ....MRS M BERSEY (Looe)
    Best Exhibit in Section E (not Class 65)
16. **The Alec Gray Perpetual Memorial Cup** ....MRS M BERSEY (Looe)
    Most points in miniature Classes
17. **The Secret Cup** ....R G SLEEMAN (Truro)
    Most points in Section E Daffodils
18. **The Daffodil Society Medal**............................. MRS M BERSEY (Looe)
    Best bloom in Class 65

Section F – HERBACEOUS
19. **The Mulock Cup** ....HELIGAN GARDENS
    Most points in Section F
20. **The Norman Knibbs Memorial Trophy** (F & G).....HELIGAN GARDENS
    Most points in Section F & G

Section G – POT PLANTS
21. **The Hodgson Challenge Cup** ....MRS J E NORMAN (Truro)
    Most points in section G

Section H – ALPINES
22. **The Cornwall Alpine Garden Society Trophy** J BOUSFIELD (Launceston)
    Most points in Section H Alpines
23. **The Patience Barnes Challenge Cup**
    (Sections A,B,C,D and H < 1/2 acre) ....MRS J COOK (Falmouth)
24. **The Bristol and West Trophy** ....L STEPHENS
    Most outstanding vase or growing plant Sections E,F,G,H.
25. **The Banksian Medal** ....R G SLEEMAN (Truro)
    Most points in Horticultural Classes (winners last 2 years ineligible)
26. **The Bickford-Smith Trophy** (Trade stands)..........R SCAMP (Falmouth)
27. **The R K Harrison Trophy Novice Classes**.......M HEDLEY (Lostwithiel)

Section K – PHOTOGRAPHY
28. **The Fortescue Cup** ....G PLATT (High Peak,Derbyshire)
    Most points in Section J
29. **The Launceston Cup** ....J LOVATT (Par)
    Best Exhibit in Section J
30. **The Goodman Challenge Cup**: B CHAMPION Head Gardener, Trelissick
    (Outstanding achievement in Cornish Horticulture)

FLORAL ART
31. **The Cornwall Theatre Of Flowers Trophy**......MRS FIONA HAMMOND
    Best Exhibit
32. **Kitson Cup:** Most points Class 148-155.................. MRS PAT KNIGHT
33. **Constance Spry Memorial Cup**.......................MRS FIONA HAMMOND
    Best Exhibit in Class 150
34. **The Margaret Shepherd Cup**...MRS B CLARK
    Best exhibit by a W I Member
35. **The Baseden Cup** ....LOOE & DISTRICT FLOWER CLUB
    Best Club or Society Exhibit in Class 147
36. **The H & M Libby Memorial Cup**................................MRS J LAWFORD
    Best Exhibit in Novice class 149

CHILDRENS SCULPTURE MADE FROM RECYCLED MATERIALS
1   ST MELLION C OF E SCHOOL
2   DOUBLETREES SCHOOL

The Cornwall Garden Society welcomes the International Camellia Society

The International Camellia Society's bi-ennial Congress is being held in England for the first time since 1982 and Falmouth has been chosen as the venue; the last one was in 2006 in Melbourne. Originally scheduled from the evening of Tuesday 1st April till the evening of Friday 4th April the UK organising committee was persuaded to extend their stay until Sunday the 6th in order to allow the 150 plus delegates to visit the CGS Spring Show at Boconnoc. Two of New Zealand's most experienced judges of camellias have even been persuaded to judge the camellia classes before dashing off to join their fellow delegates for a special evening reception at the Eden Project.

With visitors from as far afield as Australia, New Zealand, the USA, Japan and Korea, a fairly large contingent from China and others from all over Europe, this is an ideal opportunity to show off the best of Cornwall's plants and gardens and to encourage future garden tours from overseas. It is also hoped that wider publicity will be generated in Britain as a result of this event. Best of all it is a great occasion to meet keen gardeners from all over the world.

Delegates will have seen gardens that are known for their camellias such as Trewithen, Tregrehan, Tregothnan and Caerhays but we know that they are looking forward to seeing much more at Boconnoc and to meeting and "talking plants" with CGS members during the day. Rumour has it that Cornish pasties in the catering marquee are already being discussed. Anyone know how to explain these to our Chinese friends ?

Camellia x *williamsii* 'The Duchess of Cornwall'
Photo by Jim Stephens of the Duchy of Cornwall Nursery

New Cornwall Garden Society logo

It is with great pleasure that we can unveil the new logo of the CGS, an innovative and stylish design produced by Krystal Fanning at Univeristy College Falmouth. She is the winner of our competition to produce a logo; we were very impressed by the general standard of entries but Krystal's stood out for its sophisticated approach which maintained elements of our previous logo with just the right degree of modernisation. She has skillfully given an indication of a flower-head whilst not restricting her design to one specific variety. Congratulations Krystal!

Below are her own thoughts on the subject of the design brief which she was given.

My name is Krystal Fanning and I am 21 years old. I am originally from Dorset in the Southwest and have been living in Cornwall for nearly two years. I have always had a keen interest in Graphic Design, previously studying it at HND level and I'm now exploring it further doing a BA Hons at Falmouth University.

Being in the final year of the course, I am always looking for projects that inspire and provide me with the scope to explore new ideas in a range of different ways. I'm also keen to get involved with local companies, working on projects that involve the community and also ones that are sensitive to the environment. Cornwall itself has been a great inspiration to me. I have been exposed to many new exciting things, especially with being a part of the University I'm surrounded with creativity and there is still so much I haven't discovered in Cornwall. I have learned so much about things like sustainability and the environment and it's made me think about how I'm going to contribute to and work within the design world when I leave the course.

As part of the Graphic Design course there are opportunities to work on briefs set by local clients. When the Cornwall Garden Society approached the university with a brief to enhance their existing logo – almost re-inventing themselves, I saw an opportunity to work with new people, becoming involved with a society I knew little about, with the intention of making a positive difference to them. I liked the challenges that came with working with an already existing organisation – one that had established values and members within it, things I had to take into consideration whilst re-thinking their image.

Something that was a key part of this project was retaining the original essence of the Cornwall Garden Society, finding that visual balance between old and new and satisfying the existing members whilst also attracting new interest. I had become particularly aware of the values that the society holds, such as promoting, conserving and protecting the national environment in Cornwall and promoting knowledge and education in good gardening principles. These are things I wanted to amplify and I felt that the logo itself should reflect the core values of the Society and also represent others such as quality, community and passion.

The thing I liked most about working on this project was knowing I was doing something for a society very much a part of the community and one that has so much to offer people. I enjoyed working to quite a tight brief but at the same time I was able to explore different ideas and concepts – finding that final solution to suit all. Working on this project was a good experience for me because being a live brief, I obviously got to engage with clients and work to their deadlines and get some good feedback. I hope that interest in the Cornwall Garden Society continues to grow and that I have made a positive difference.

CONSERVING HERITAGE PLANTS THROUGH MICROPROPAGATION

The origins of Cornwall's historic plants.

by Ros Smith B.Sc
Manager of the micropropagation unit at Duchy College, Rosewarne, Camborne
Photos by the author unless stated

The historic gardens of Cornwall contain a unique heritage of plant species brought into this country from around the mid 1800s by early plant hunters such as Sir Joseph Dalton Hooker. Following his expeditions to Sikkim he returned with seed of Rhododendrons such as *falconeri, griffithianum and thomsonii* (i). The mild climate of Cornwall was ideal for trialling such exotic finds which were not believed to be hardy in other parts of the country. The seedlings were grown on by his Cornish friends at Tremough, Carclew, Burncoose and Penjerrick and from there were moved between gardens through family connections, for example Mr. Robert Were Fox sent plants from Penjerrick to Glendurgan and Trebah. Some of these original rhododendrons grown from Sir Joseph Hooker's seeds can still be found in the walled garden at Tremough. In due course the head gardeners used these species to breed ever more colourful and interesting hybrids. There was, at that time, great rivalry between the head gardeners and indeed estate owners to produce bigger flower trusses and better colours. At Tremough (ii) the owner William Shilson, a keen horticulturalist, and his head gardener Richard Gill were very successful and produced numerous hybrids around the 1900s. The RHS Award of Merit was awarded to no less than nine hybrids bred there, one of which 'Shilsonii' commemorates the owner. Another hybrid 'Beauty of Tremough' is named after the estate, and was awarded a RHS First Class Certificate in 1902. At one time Richard Gill was believed to hold the largest stock of hybrid rhododendrons in the world. Many of the Cornish gardens were originally planted with rhododendrons purchased from Tremough.

A more detailed report on the history of early Cornish rhododendron growing has been written by Walter Magor (iii). We now reap the benefit from such early introductions as can be seen in the glorious displays of rhododendrons, magnolias and camellias which epitomise the Cornish Spring gardens and are such an attraction for the early season tourist. The picture above shows the glorious *R. arboreum* in flower at Tregothnan. ➡

There are also natural reasons for the loss of historic plants.

The earliest rhododendron plantings are more than 150 years old now and their lifespan is unknown. It could be that some are nearing the end of their life and others may already have gone. What is known is that plants lose their vigour as they age. They may become weakened and less resilient to the vagaries of the British climate. In recent years there have been unusual weather patterns, the most notable being the gales of 1987 which caused general devastation across the county. One would expect these ancient plants to cope less ably in such situations. Plate 2 shows a bank of Rhododendron hybrids at Carclew.

Plants lost through disease.

A recent problem has arisen, seemingly more devastating to the gardens than that of the storms. It is the outbreak of a fungal disease which can easily spread through susceptible plants, resulting in their death. The disease is commonly known as 'Sudden Oak Death' after its effect on the Tanoak (Lithocarpus densiflorus) of California and is caused by a fungus named Phytophthora ramorum. A more localised species, P. kernoviae, has been associated with Cornish woodland settings. (Vegetable gardeners will be familiar with the rapid spread of Potato Blight which is caused by another species Phytophthora infestans. It would seem to be that the humid and moist conditions in Cornwall are ideal for both life cycles. Unfortunately, the host range of both of these fungi encompasses the major players of the spring garden display; Rhododendron, Magnolia and Camellia. A full host list and more detailed information can be found on the Defra website: http://www.defra.gov.uk.planth/phytophthora.

The principal symptoms of P.ramorum infection on rhododendrons can be described as leaf blight (browning or blackening) and sudden shoot dieback. Rhododendrons, however, can be affected by a number of different Phytophthora species and root invading diseases which cause similar symptoms. One should not, therefore, automatically assume that because a rhododendron is dying it has succumbed to Sudden Oak Death. As mentioned previously, the excesses of rain and unseasonable dry spells can cause great stress to both young and old plants alike.

The species Rhododendron ponticum has been traditionally used by many estates as a windbreak around the ornamental garden and as an understorey in woodland situations. The widespread distribution of this species and its susceptibility to P.ramorum/kernoviae has resulted in its removal where possible in order to reduce the risk of infecting the more important rhododendron species and hybrids and other valuable plant species. Those gardens open to the public have responded promptly to this threat and large swathes of R. ponticum have been removed. →

Locating the originals.

It is sometimes difficult to track down the original plants for a variety of reasons. Many of the historic gardens have changed ownership throughout the years and no longer remain in the hands of the same family. As a result of this the planting plans and records have often been destroyed or lost when the property changed hands. Unless one has expert knowledge, it is often difficult to be certain that the rhododendron hybrid pointed out as 'X' is correctly identified when it should really be the one further along the border!

Another reason may be that those inheriting an historic garden do not share the enthusiasm for plants as did their earlier ancestors. Historic specimens may be chopped down unknowingly because they look untidy and replaced by more modern plantings.

In the years following the first world war, some gardens became run down and neglected. So many of the gardening staff did not return from active service that gardens became difficult to maintain. Financial problems too meant that the funds were not available to employ the quantity of gardeners as in pre-war days. Nature gradually reclaimed the furthest areas resulting in an encroaching jungle of overgrown rhododendrons and brambles. I am sure everyone is familiar with the 'finding' of the 'Lost Gardens of Heligan.' The historic plantings there have been secured by virtue of the area becoming a tourist attraction. Who can fail to be impressed by the towering masses of colour from the rhododendron flowers and the delicate looking magnolia blossoms?

There is the possibility that historic plants can disappear when land is sold off for development. The developer wants to maximise his return and will not be at all upset if the ground workers should clear most of the specimen plants too. It takes a lot of effort to retain individual plants on a site and anyway, they can stick something back there when they have finished can't they?

The result is that new vistas have been created which may not have been seen since the time of the original plantings. The lower branches of some of the ornamental rhododendrons have also been removed and densely planted areas 'opened up'. This gives greater air movement throughout the area which prevents the static humidity ideal for spore germination. Leaf litter is removed where possible to lessen the risk of the inoculum surviving through the winter. These procedures are something that gardeners can do at home in order to reduce the risk of infection.

This may all seem to be 'doom and gloom' for the ancient Cornish garden plants. But all will not be lost! A laboratory procedure can take small pieces of plant such as shoots or even flowers and regenerate numerous whole plants again. It is not magic; it is done by the appliance of science!

The micropropagation process

Put simply, small pieces of plant material such as tiny shoots are surface cleaned and grown in a sterile nutrient jelly at a constant temperature under artificial lighting.

The aim is to force the immature/dormant buds into growth and produce multiple shoots which can then be encouraged to proliferate further.

It is possible that one shoot could provide thousands more (clones) within a year or so. The process is much more complicated, however, and there are many hazards along the way, the main problem being the removal of contaminants which otherwise compete with the cutting for food.

At home, when plants are propagated from cuttings a reasonable degree of cleanliness is needed to prevent their loss through disease and decay. The micropropagation process, however, requires that all plant surfaces be completely free of any fungus, bacteria and algae which are naturally present in large quantities, especially on older plants. The chemical sodium hypochlorite, found in household bleach, is used in various dilutions and for various lengths of immersion. Such careful preparation is required because the nutrient jelly also contains sugar, the energy source for the cutting, which is also the ideal substrate for these contaminants to grow on. Consider what happens to your jar of jam once opened and then forgotten in the back of a cupboard. Even the cleanest of kitchens have fungal spores in the air which are invisible to our eyes! →

The magic ingredients in the nutrient jelly, if they can be described as such, are the plant growth hormones which are responsible for the development of shoots or roots. Their application is under human control so that cuttings can be programmed to produce quantities of shoots and then by changing the type of hormone can be made to root.

The whole process thus involves a number of different stages: the cleaning stage, the multiplication of shoots, their rooting and finally their acclimatisation to outdoor conditions. Plates 3 - 8 show this progression with young rhododendron shoots leading to a well established plant. In theory any plant can be micropropagated but in practice there are some that stubbornly refuse to respond. Similarly there are plants in the garden that are fussy about their growing conditions. The micropropagation process does however allow more intensive treatment to be applied to encourage bud development.

In 2004 a financial donation from Heligan Gardens was used to start a conservation program for their extensive collection of rhododendrons. It had been noticed that some were not putting on much annual growth and were generally looking frail. Micropropagation was chosen because it can overcome the difficulty of rooting shoots from ancient plants and it also results in the production of many plants from a little original material. Young vegetative shoots were taken but proved difficult to decontaminate, probably due to the quantity of fungi and algae embedded in the surrounding bark. The idea of protecting the developing young shoots with flower sleeves proved a little more successful and caused great interest to the public as they walked around the gardens. It was in the following year, 2005, that Duchy College was successful with a bid for European funding to expand the project and conserve more rare plant species threatened by Phytophthora ramorum. →

4

5

6

7

8

Defra were also very supportive with funding and the laboratory was granted a licence to allow infected material to be processed in the hope of saving special plants from possible extinction. In the early days of P.ramorum control it was thought that complete destruction of the plant was necessary to prevent its spread.

The scope of the project also enabled student researchers to be taken on to work on the micropropagation of other susceptible host plants such as magnolia, camellia and rare trees.
The scanning of scientific journals via the internet produced another possible source of plant tissue that could be used for micropropagation. It was a source of tissue which could be more successfully decontaminated and was also available over a longer period of time. It was found that by tweaking the formulation slightly and adapting the methodology many more plants could be successfully grown in culture. The tissue used is the floral bud, which in the rhododendron is tightly covered by scale leaves. When it is taken at the correct stage, a strong decontaminant can be applied without fear of damaging the developing flowers within. The individual florets complete with stalks (pedicel) can then be dissected out under sterile conditions and treated with a particular plant growth hormone.

After a few months in culture tiny shoots appear from the pedicel and rapidly develop. Plates 9 - 12 show the procedure and results when using rhododendron flowers. One floret may give rise to thirty shoots. There may be up to twenty florets within a bud, therefore there could be a potential six hundred plantlets from one floral bud. In reality there is often latent contamination by algae and bacteria which cuts down the numbers of successful florets. This technique is a faster method of increasing cloned material than the traditional micropropagation method of starting with vegetative shoots. It has also proved to be a more successful method for decontamination. This can be illustrated by the difficulty of micropropagating *R. macabeanum*. This beautiful large leaved rhododendron is found in several old Cornish gardens and flowers in slightly different shades of creamy yellow. →

There are especially good forms of this species in the gardens of Trengwainton (Plate 13) and Trewithen (Plate 14). Trengwainton Gardens also has a cluster of *R. macabeanum* plants originating from the same seed pod which were collected by Frank Kingdom-Ward. The flowers display slight variation in colouration, and two are particularly fine. *R. macabeanum* also exhibits wonderful pink colouring on the young growth in late spring. Successful propagation from cuttings is very difficult to achieve, therefore young vegetative shoots were collected for micropropagation in 2005. The shoots are covered in thick silky hairs which unfortunately trap anything coming into contact with them. Despite an intense scrubbing with a tooth brush (new!) and antibacterial hand-wash, it proved impossible to decontaminate a number of shoots and micropropagation was abandoned for that year. The following year some flower buds were removed in late January and rigorously decontaminated. The florets were clean but did not survive. Last spring, 2007, it proved to be third time lucky. Floral buds were collected a little later in their development and processed as previously. By the autumn there were many tiny shoots appearing around the flower stems (see plate 15).

By summer 2008 there should be plantlets ready for potting on from two of the Trengwainton forms. These can then be distributed to aid in their long term conservation. More than 350 rhododendron plants have been processed so far from sixteen Cornish gardens. The success rate of over 70% goes some way to ensure that important rhododendrons are saved for future generations.

Research will continue provided sufficient funding can be sourced to support the project. Work is required to improve on this success rate and also focus on other plant species under threat. A total of 27 Magnolia species and hybrids have been processed from vegetative shoots with some success. Again some of them suffer from the problem of hairy shoots!

Twenty other important plant introductions which are under threat of the disease have been processed, again with mixed results. Much time and effort is needed to source or devise a suitable nutrient jelly for each new genus of plant. They are as fussy over their food as human beings!

Bibliography:

(i). Sir Joseph Dalton Hooker – Traveller and Plant Collector, by Ray Desmond, Antique Collectors' Club, 1999.
ISBN 1-85149-305-0

(ii). Tremough, Penryn – The Historic Estate, by Margaret Grose and Shiona King, MH&GM Grose, 2003.
ISBN 0-9545337-0-4

(iii). Magor W. The Early Days of Rhododendron Growing in Cornwall.
Journal of the Cornwall Garden Society No.30 March 1987

Photographic acknowledgements:

Plate 1 by kind permission of Ian Wright, head gardener, Trengwainton Gardens.
Plate 2 by kind permission of Garry Long, head gardener, Trewithen Gardens.
Plates 3 - 14 by Ros Smith.

Contact details for Ros Smith:
Telephone number 01209 722138
E-mail address ros.smith@duchy.ac.uk

BBC Radio Cornwall Gardenline
Tim Hubbard
Photos by Charles Francis

Radio car at Boconnoc for the CGS Spring Flower Show 2007

Tim Hubbard, who will be familiar to everyone as presenter of his Sunday morning programme Gardenline, recalls some experiences from his long career with our local BBC station.

Sundays 9.00 am to 12.00 noon 103.9 and 95.2 FM

I've been lucky enough to work on gardening programmes on BBC Radio Cornwall for a number of years now. You'll remember Jack Andrews's chats with Chris Blount many years ago and I spent many happy recording sessions out with Jack in his garden. His enthusiasm must have been contagious because I then went on to work for many seasons with David Pearce, David Johnson and Philip McMillan Browse. Amongst other things we took a 'Gardeners' Question Time' style programme out on the road visiting gardening clubs all over Cornwall.

This, in turn, led to some question and answer sessions tied in with tours of some of Cornwall's National Trust gardens. Head Gardeners at Trengwainton, St Michael's Mount, Trelissick, Cothele and Lanhydrock showed groups of gardening experts and listeners around the gardens, we had supper and then recorded some of my favourite BBC Radio Cornwall programmes ever.

Tim interviewing at Boconnoc 2007

For the past few years I've been working with the wonderful team of Tracy Wilson, Alistair Rivers, John Harris and Nigel Pascoe. On Sunday mornings, starting at 9.00am and ably backed up with "guest appearances" from Barry Champion we've tackled questions about slugs and salvias, greenhouses and gunnera and bananas and bonsai.

Opening the weekly postbag is always an exciting discovery. As well as phone calls (on 01872 222222), emails (to tim.hubbard@bbc.co.uk) letters come in thick and fast (to Gardenline, BBC Radio Cornwall, Phoenix Wharf, Truro, TR1 1UA). Some contain photographs and some detailed description but the most interesting contain pieces of plant material. By and large, though, much of it is unusable; listeners forget that a whole week elapses between each programme and so greenery either rots, dessicates or dies which makes the expert's job so much the harder.

One of the main highlights of the past couple of years was winning a silver medal at the Royal Horticultural Society's Hampton Court Palace Flower Show. Along with the Gardens of Cornwall project – part of Cornwall Enterprise - we organised a competition for amateur listeners to submit a design which – for them – summed up "A Garden of Cornwall". After sifting through hundreds of entries the winner was Louise Todd from Lelant. The simplicity of her sophisticated design appealed to the judges because it blended a hot dry courtyard with tropical jungle combined with an overall feel of the seaside.

Louise's design was literally brought to life by the four BBC expert gardeners and myself – working in the 30 degree heat of the summer of 2006. Some days it was hard to tell which looked the more tired and wilted – the plants or the people. After a huge amount of effort the garden looked stunning and featured a stunning piece of glass sculpture by Penryn's Malcolm Sutcliffe . It was officially opened by Gloria Hunniford along with Sir Cliff Richard and then the gates opened to hundreds of thousands of garden lovers. Judicious tweaking and dead heading along with pretty constant watering to combat the summer heat made sure that the garden looked its best until – on the last day – the bell rang, the big sell off began and the garden was destroyed. It seemed strange to see the grass underneath the whole thing looking pretty much as it had done just one week earlier.

A second category of the competition saw three students from Redruth School win the chance to design a planting scheme for the Cornwall County Council roundabout which is part of the new Devoran bypass near Truro. Planting took place in February 2007. Due to various complications parts of the design are yet to be realised but already the water-inspired central planting of grasses is wafting in the breeze like fronds of seaweed and the Mediterranean *Phoenix canariensis* are hinting at the delights of the sub tropical gardens waiting around Falmouth and the shores of the Helford.

Gardenline is there to help every gardener in Cornwall and on the rare occasions when the experts don't know then we can always rely on other listeners coming up with their own solution. Join us on the radio (103.9 and 95.2FM) every Sunday morning between 9.00am and 12 noon or call 01872 22 22 22.

To Dig
or
not to dig?

That is the question

by Eric Milner Kay

Double digging in the Lost Gardens of Heligan
Photo Charles Francis

To most gardeners, pleasure comes when plants bloom, doubtful starters survive, fruit ripens and vegetables flourish in abundance. But this is the result of a lot of hard work which has borne down heavily, particularly on those who annually continue to dig their gardens. And is all this labour necessary? The debate 'to dig or not to dig' is a perennial in gardening circles and is very relevant to the maintenance of flower beds and herbaceous borders throughout the seasons; many would wish not to do any more than is necessary.

Basics involved:

As has often been said, soil is not just dead dirt, but a complex mix formed of the inorganic weathered fragments of the underlying rock together with the activity of a multitude of living organisms and the climate of the region. It is the vital bridge between the dead (inorganic) and the living (organic) world on which nearly all terrestrial life depends.

A medieval (mid twelfth century) stained glass window in Canterbury Cathedral shows Adam digging in his garden. The blade of the shovel is the traditional Celtic heart shape still in use here in Cornwall also in Brittany, parts of Wales, the Islands and Highlands of Scotland, but it has a short shaft and a handle like the modern spade.
(reproduced by kind permission of the Cathedral authorities)

Lichen colonising the granite of Harry's Walls Hugh Town, St Mary's, Isles of Scilly
Photo Eric Milner Kay

In the long evolution of the earth's green mantle, the first recognisable fossil soils appear some 440 million years ago (mya) long after the beginning of life in the ancient seas some 3,500 mya. Initially the freshly exposed bare rock surfaces did not provide suitable conditions for colonisation by plants. Lengthy periods of weathering were needed including fragmentation of the rock, often by extreme temperature changes; atmospheric changes with abundance of carbon dioxide (CO_2) and acid rains; increasing levels of oxygen; organic acids prduced by invading bacteria and eventually plant growth in the form of lichens, the early colonisers. The fossil soil profiles of 440 mya gives evidence of the long period of their development, with oxidation of organic matter and deep penetration by burrowing organisms, thus providing stability for their root systems, essential for plant colonisation and growth. As vegetation increased, soil accumulation became much more rapid, for long periods more than the present day. (see Fig. 1) →

Crab's Eye Lichen *(Ochrolechia parella)* colonising the Pillow Lavas of Pentire Point, Cornwall
Photo Eric Milner Kay

Fig 1
A diagram to illustrate the interaction of climate, biological activity and the bed rock in the production of soils.

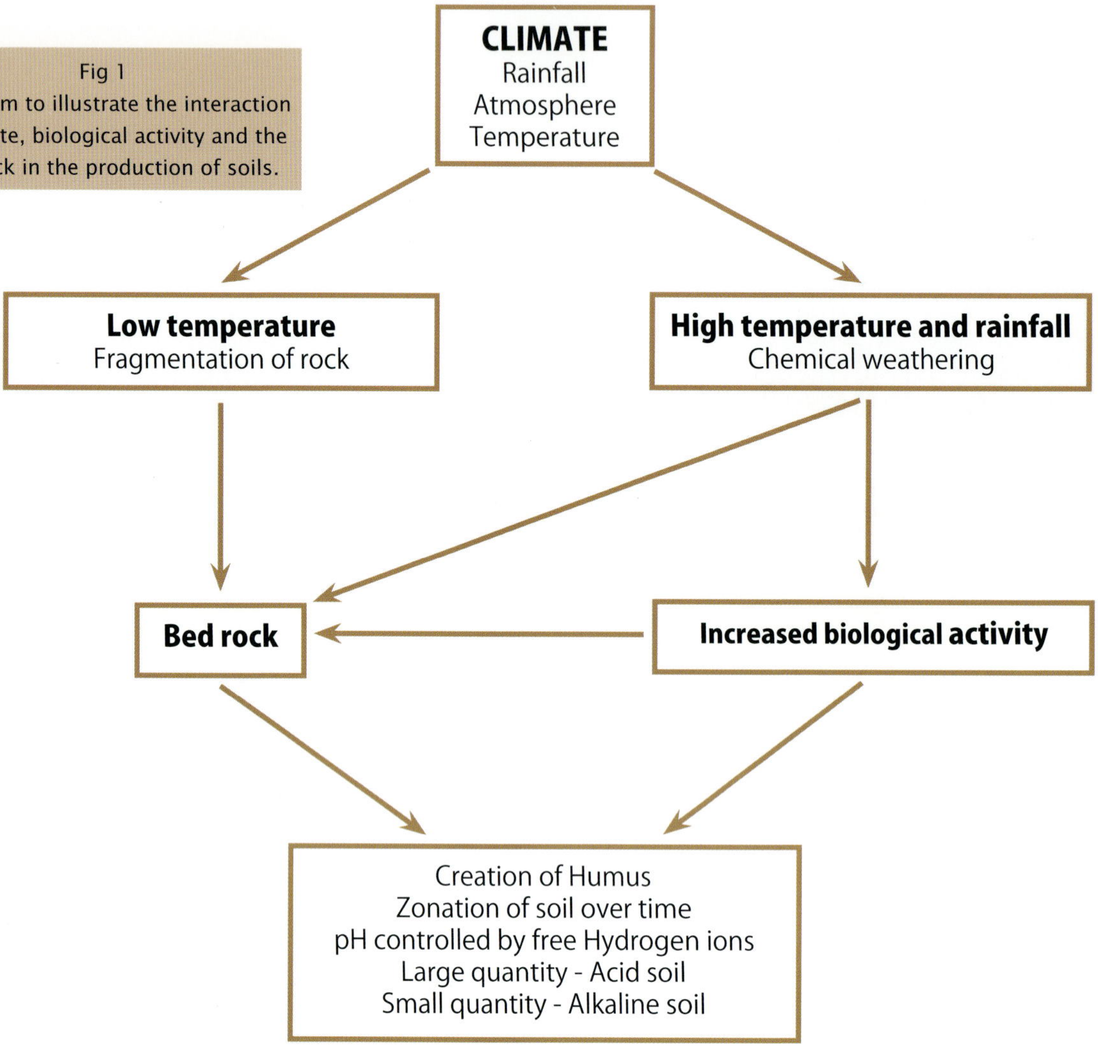

CLIMATE
Rainfall
Atmosphere
Temperature

Low temperature
Fragmentation of rock

High temperature and rainfall
Chemical weathering

Bed rock

Increased biological activity

Creation of Humus
Zonation of soil over time
pH controlled by free Hydrogen ions
Large quantity - Acid soil
Small quantity - Alkaline soil

Apart from the granite of the high moors, where thin peaty soils and blanket bogs are found, and the Lizard complex, possibly of pre-Cambrian age, the location of most of our gardens are underlain by Carboniferous (290-360 million years) and Devonian (360-400 my) sedimentary rocks. These lie, as bed rock, below the soils east/west across the county. Many areas are overlain by Coombe rock, formed during the freeze/thaw activity of the last ice age and give rise to acid Brown Earth loamy soils in the well-drained areas, often containing fragments of rock but little influenced by the nature of the bed rock.

Over successive generations, gardeners have enriched these with bulk manures to increase productivity and whilst an idealised soil profile shows various horizons (see Fig. 2) it is the top few inches which are the most important for plant growth. The transition from one horizon to another can be indistinct, especially in well cultivated or shallow soils. →
Fig. 2

Two soil profiles to horizon C at Furzeball, Cornwall, both on the Dartmouth Beds of Old Red Sandstones (a) in the area of kitchen garden dug for several centuries, to accumulate soil from manure and human waste to a depth of 2ft (0.6m) and (b) opened from a field 21 years ago with thin soil c. 6 inches deep, now with annual addition of compost some 10 inches (15cm) deep. Photos by Eric Milner Kay.
The narrow bands on the scale are cm, the wider ones inches. Total 6 inches (15cm).

HORIZON — HUMUS Zone of intense biological activity
A — Leached soil. Little organic activity. Mineral particles
B — Enriched with soluble minerals often iron oxides and clay
C — Weathered rock
D — BED ROCK

It is in this zone, as mentioned above, that the dynamic mixing of the inorganic and organic occurs to produce soil by the activity organisms, such as worms, ground beetles and the hidden multitude of bacteria which convert the proteins of dead plants and animals into nitrates essential for plant growth and leaf formation. Soils also need pore spaces to allow the free movement of gases to aerate root systems with oxygen (O^2) and to discharge carbon dioxide (CO^2) to the atmosphere. Compaction of the soil, often by needless trampling, prevents this and inhibits the growth of the plant, which ideally should contain, in any volume of soil: 25% water, 45% mineral particles, 25% air and some 5% of organic matter.

Digging-in green manure
Photo Charles Francis

In the past, annual digging incorporating bulk manure was seen as the only way to create fertile soils with an open-pored crumb structure. It also meant that dead plants and weeds (green manure) were turned into the soil and plant pests and/or their eggs were exposed to predators. But it also exposed beneficial organisms to the same predators (mainly birds). In recent years research has now revealed all the trillions of previously unseen micro-organisms which make up the structure of the soil, in addition to those we see every day. In fact, with the aid of the electron microscope*, it can be seen that a speck of garden soil can contain up to a million bacteria and the garden some millions of microscopic forms of mites, soil scorpions, ticks and a variety of fungi. Obviously amongst these, in any garden, some are beneficial, e.g. Rhizobium bacteria, fixing nitrogen from the air, and others spreading unwelcome plant dieases e.g. Armillaria mella, 'Honey fungus', and Botrytis cinerea the grey mould fungus. ➝

* for some details see vol. 50 of the Journal (2007) pp.33-38.

Amanita Muscaria
Photo Charles Francis

However, many plant problems prove less of a menace where the soil is rich in organic material (compost and manures), with a good aerated crumb structure, which helps to establish a balanced community of micro-organisms near the surface. This also includes unseen species of fungi, these live in a symbiotic relationship with many bushes and trees, both plant and fungi often gaining from the association. Fungi lack the pigment chlorophyll so cannot synthesise their own food from sunlight and many species gain sustenance by living off dead vegetation, helping in the process of decomposition, or on living plants. The vegetative part of fungi, the mycelium, forms branching colonies of filamentous cells which attach themselves to the living roots of trees and bushes by penetrating the cells of their root cortex. This forms a dense and extensive mantle around the plant, known as the mycorrhiza, through which the exchange of food from the plant to the fungi and water and nutrient minerals - phosphorous and nitrogen - from the soil/fungi pass to the plant.

Some help a variety of herbaceous plants, for example, the poisonous Fly Agaric, *Amanita muscaria*, (above) forms a mycorrhizal mat with conifers, birch and sometimes beech, endotropic mycorrhiza attach to orchids and to the Ericaceae, but *Boletus elegans* (right) is more specific to larch. The fungi thus extends the root system over a much wider area and can be of great benefit for the plant, but these are physically very fragile and very sensitive to all kinds of garden fungicides. ➔

Boletus elegans
Photo Lara Stefansdottir

THE CORNISH GARDEN

Photo Charles Francis

To Dig or Not to Dig?

From the above it can be seen that the soil is a very complex mixture of minerals and living organisms and the aim must be to establish the right balance to maintain its fertility and the health of all the plants in cultivation. Clearly this complexity would suggest that there can be no single rule for the whole garden.

Where shrubs and trees dominate, the soil should not be disturbed by deep digging which would destroy the delicate spread of the fungal mycorrhiza thus starving the plant of vital water and minerals and resulting in the wilt often seen where digging has been too close. A mulch spread of compost in the spring will help, particularly round shallow rooted shrubs like rhododendrons and azaleas. The soil organisms will do the rest by carrying it down to the root area of the plants. Similarly, flower beds where annuals are grown will benefit from mulching plus a light hoeing where necessary to kill off unwanted weeds, herbicides should be avoided. Close planting and ground cover plants will help to reduce weed growth.

Annual vegetables are not as dependent on many soil organisms but possibly more on the structure and mineral content of the soil. Occasionally in a vegetable garden, and to establish a garden in a newly built housing estate, benefit could come from deep digging to loosen the soil and bring nearer to the surface many of the minerals leeched from the upper layers over the years. This activity allows for the introduction of bulk manures and provides an opportunity, where necessary, to adjust the pH. of the soil.

Most ornamentals thrive in our slightly acid soils but a number of vegetables e.g. the brassica family, benefit from the introduction of garden lime well in advance of planting, but not at the same time as manure. It reacts with nitrogen-rich manures releasing nitrogen, as well as ammonia, and may damage nearby plants. Lime no more than once every two years. The less the soil is trampled on the better and, again, it is best to avoid herbicides when cultivating.

Soil pH

Comparatively cheap meters are now available to measure the pH of soils, perhaps less accurate but certainly easier to read than the old testing kits and colour charts.
These read hydrogen ion concentration suspended in soil water on a pH scale of 0 to 14, borrowed from chemistry, the lower the number the more acid, the higher the number the more alkaline, mid 7 being neutral. This is a logarithmic scale so that each unit above or below 7 means a ten-fold increase, thus a reading of 5 will indicate that the soil is 100 times more acid than neutral.
Where soils have formed on limestone and/or chalk they are normally alkaline and are acid on sandstones, shales, conglomerates and most igneous rocks. Nutrients absorbed from the soil by plants, in solution, is more readily available in acidic soils which are also beneficial for the micro-organisms involved in the conversion of dead vegetation and other organic matter into humus. This provides a slow release of nitrogen, phosphates and other minerals to the roots of plants, a transfer which becomes increasingly more restricted with increasing alkalinity.

⋄ Eric Milner Kay is a member of the Cornwall Garden Society.
⋄ The author wishes to thank his daughter, Bridget, for her careful preparation of the manuscript for publication.

Further reading:

Pears Pauline:	Encyclopaedia of Organic Gardening.	
	Henry Doubleday Research Association/Dorling Kindersley	
Readman Jo:	Soil Care and Management	H.D.R.A./Search Press
Dowding C:	Organic Gardening	R.H.S.
	The Natural No-Dig Way	

Note - Mycorrhizal fungi is available in powder form, from many larger garden centres.

Lanterns Garden Near Mylor

Fund-raising for Precious Lives Appeal

by Heather Hall

photos by Charles Francis

The other day someone asked me:

'So, what is so special about Lanterns Garden?'

I suppose it all began for me when I lived here in the mid-1960s. Then it was just like any other uncultivated plot of land, a wilderness of brambles, nettles, wild garlic, buttercups, docks, weeds, willows and fallen oak that had taken over an exceptionally boggy, east-facing valley. All manner of birds and wildlife flourished unobserved. The streams and subterranean springs that had surfaced, had no proper channels to run through. There were no paths or flat areas of firm, raised ground to stand on. The only dry land was a small disused Killas slate quarry which rose almost vertically for about 30 feet on the west boundary of the plot. Below the quarry to the south side there was, and still is, a sunken reservoir fed by subterranean spring water. Before mains water was piped to Restronguet Hill, this was the supply of drinking water for the area. Even today some local residents only use the spring water. It is carried to them in pipes running under Lanterns Garden.

When my parents, Douglas and Irene Chapman, retired in the 1970s, their plans to develop the garden started in earnest. First of all, they made new channels for the streams and springs to tumble along. The water ran through the land from several directions, so this was not as easy to do as it sounds. They started by making a zig-zag path beside a fallen oak trunk which in turn made a stream boundary. Then they constructed small bridges to cross over some of the flowing water and in one place the water was piped out of sight under a concrete raft.

Next, winding paths were laid to follow the streams. In some places small steps were needed to connect the various path levels. Raised beds began to take shape and some beds needed walls for support. Then Doug turned his attention to building greenhouses and a potting shed. He ensured that all rainwater from gutters went into waterbutts outside and inside the greenhouses and the potting shed. I am so grateful that I don't have to carry cans of water when plants in the greenhouse pots dry out. Up till now, I have never had to water the garden!

Irene started on the planting. She began gardening around the house. It stands on the floor of the old Killas slate quarry. She used 2 buckets and a pickaxe. The buckets held compost and mulch. The pickaxe was used to get stones and slate up. The stones went into the boggy parts of the surrounding clay-floored land. The compost and mulch went into the holes she'd made with the pickaxe. Then she'd poke in cuttings, or put in the small plants she'd either grown from seed or cuttings, or collected from friends. I remember being told to be careful not to tread on a tiny two inch high tree. I didn't and it's now grown to about 30 feet. My mother was a very knowledgeable and enthusiastic, horticulturalist. I should have learnt a lot about gardening. Sad to say, my interests at the time went firmly in other directions. I liked a pretty garden to sit in but had scant understanding of how to make it so. When I returned to live at Lanterns in 2000, I hardly knew where to begin!

Visitors kept asking me, 'What's that called?' and of course I didn't know. All the labels had either faded or fallen off. Nothing had a name that I could use to research the plant's needs. Something had to flower before I could attempt to try to track it down in a picture book, I didn't know whether, when, what or how, to feed, prune or remove.

Luckily, people kept coming to see the garden and to buy Irene's plants. So I asked my garden visitors if they knew what things were called. Sometimes they could advise me and I'm so grateful to have had their help. As Lanterns had been empty for a while, it was very overgrown when I came back. At first there was a tremendous amount of pruning and removal of dead wood needed. The paths had to be cleared. New springs had emerged and water appeared to be taking over the garden beds again in several places. Some of the paths and bridges had to be raised and new channels dug. Then I began to run out of plants to sell. Those Irene had propagated were diminishing, so after scanning several more books I started trying to propagate from the stock. At first there were some spectacular failures and equally surprising successes. Fortunately I'm getting more consistent results now. →

> **THE GARDEN AND HOUSE PLANTS ARE FOR SALE IN AID OF THE CHARITY**
> ## CHILDREN'S HOSPICE SOUTHWEST 'PRECIOUS LIVES APPEAL'
> **WHICH IS RAISING FUNDS FOR A CHILDREN'S HOSPICE IN CORNWALL.**

The view down towards Restronguet Creek near Pandora Inn

My mother wrote reams of gardening notes, lists, hints and diaries. I've recently plucked up the courage to try to tackle her monthly 'To Do' lists. I really enjoy trying to follow them through, even though I often fail to keep up. I face the challenge and lose to Mother Nature regularly, especially after May when everything races upwards and southwards at an impossible rate.

Still the question remains:

'What makes Lanterns so special?'

Maybe it's because it's packed with plants and has year round interest and colour.

Maybe it has something to do with the fact that some of its visitors return year by year, season by season, even from abroad and we talk and exchange ideas and plants.

Many visitors tell me what a magical and inspirational garden Lanterns is. They say they like coming for its peace, tranquility and relaxation.

Maybe it's special because it's not neat and tidy everywhere and it definitely says 'there's work in progress here'. Some visitors have told me they prefer the more tangled growth. It enables them to relate Lanterns to their own gardens. Mine is certainly not a 'Show-Garden,' parts are more like a lost and interesting jungle! See the Visitors' Book, below.

One of the reasons I find Lanterns special is because, even after all these years of being in the garden nearly every day, I often have the joy and surprise of seeing something growing or flowering that I've never ever noticed. It may catch my eye at ground level or be waving at me from the tree tops. I wonder why I have not seen it before. Also, I really enjoy the moment when another plant, shrub or tree is named by an appreciative visiting gardener. One such identification was of the stunningly beautiful *Rhododendron* 'Loderi King George', with its fantastic perfume and its huge spread of massive blooms sprawling across the south boundary stream.

Another tree, special to me, is of course, the little palm tree I didn't step on. It's grown to be a 30 foot *Trachycarpus fortunei*. It's amazing to remember that it came here from St. Mawes in a two-inch pot in 1970.

Perhaps I should choose the huge Loquat as my most special tree. It arrived here as a seed that I'd stuck in an airmail letter written to my mother from Cyprus in 1971.

Next to the Loquat is a wonderful *Acer palmatum atropurpureum*, below. This was also grown from seed and I knew it's mother tree when I was a little girl. →

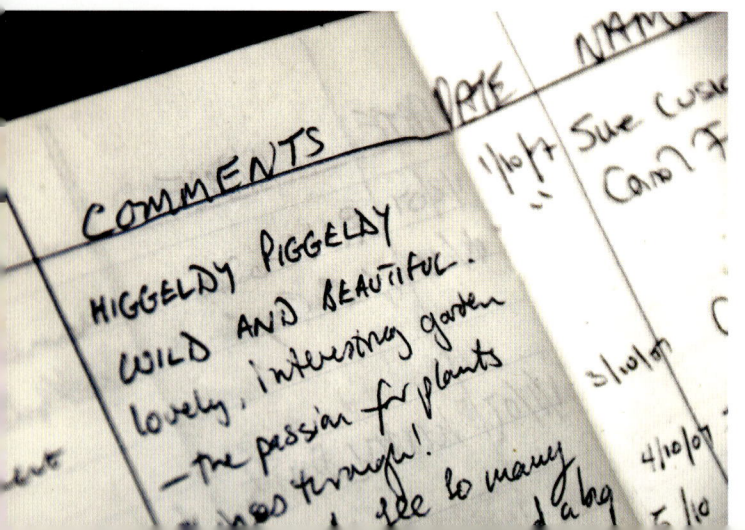

Acer palmatum atropurpureum

The tall Metasequoia and the abundantly climbing wisterias I remember as tiny cuttings. I find it impossible to choose just one favourite, special, thing about this garden. The fact is, many of the large flowering trees and established shrubs here were grown from seeds or tiny cuttings taken from other gardens I grew up in. Many now can provide support for the climbers which grow up, in and among them, in a mostly, friendly way. There are too many different species to list here properly, some have been identified and have new labels, whilst others are still puzzling me. One mystery for example is a camellia. It resembles a huge, pink, double-headed waterlily. Maybe next year some knowledgeable, interested, visitor will be able to tell me its name.

I should also mention that the top of the garden is looking less well established. This is because on January 18th 2007, storms brought down, two 70 foot Larch trees. They smashed and damaged everything in their path. Replanting the area has been my main challenge this year and the work is still in progress. One visitor-gardener surveyed the destruction and told me quite firmly: 'That's one of the joys, gardens are always changing!' Mother would have probably agreed.

I hope I've tempted you to come here and see for yourself. Maybe you'll find it a different kind of garden-visit experience and perhaps you will tell me 'What's so special about Lanterns.' You can certainly appreciate not having to walk long distances to see a wide variety of some natural and some special plantings for different growing conditions. The garden was landscaped and developed from 1973 to ensure a seasonal succession of flower and foliage, colour and fragrance. Most of the plants started living here as very small, young specimens but the rate of growth in this boggy valley has been astounding.

Abutilon megapotamicum

WE ARE OPEN DAILY THROUGHOUT THE YEAR from 11am till dusk.

Follow signs to Mylor Bridge from the (A39) Truro to Falmouth road
From Mylor Bridge follow the 'Pandora Inn' signs leading you down Restronguet Hill
Lanterns is on the right approx 250 yds up from the waterfront.
Yellow signs mark the short drive into the garden.
There is limited parking.

Most of the garden paths are unsuitable for wheelchairs.

All entrance donations and money for plants purchased can be put in the collection box on the garage wall. Entrance is by donation in aid of the
'PRECIOUS LIVES APPEAL'.

Plants are also for sale in aid of this children's hospice charity and include: special foliage and flowering perennials for sun, shade, waterside and dry conditions, sturdy young trees, shrubs and climbers, both evergreen and deciduous indoor plants for year round interest in house or conservatory.

Dogs on leads are welcome.

No-one has stepped into the streams by mistake yet but there could always be a first time. So please be careful. Watch where you place your feet as you go along the twisty paths and enjoy a very special small garden.

Camellia Kelvingtoniana

THIS SPORTING LIFE

TEXT & PHOTOS BY BEE ROBSON

Photo Julian Stephens

BEE ROBSON LOOKS AT HOW CAMELLIA CULTIVARS ARE CREATED FROM SPORTS

Bee Robson is an history graduate and Curator of the National Collection of Camellias and Rhododendrons at the Lost Gardens of Heligan.

Camellias first came into this country as live plants in the mid-18th century; the earliest known was a single red belonging to Lord Petrie that bloomed at Thornton Hall in Essex in 1739. As far as we know this was an isolated import and remained so for the next fifty years but if no more plants came in from abroad, single red camellias were being propagated and sold in this country. William Curtis, a London nursery-man, was raising and selling these plants but only in very small quantities. Curtis had recently founded what would become one of the most important botanical and horticultural periodicals of the next fifty years, *The Botanical Magazine*, and in 1788 he published a painting by Sowerby of The Rose Camellia. He noted in his text that *"the Camellia is generally treated as a stove plant,"* but it seems *"one of the properest plants imaginable for the conservatory,"* and goes on to say that *"the high price at which it has hitherto been sold"* has prevented it being *"hazarded"* as an outdoor plant. This explains the very small numbers of plants produced. Regarded as stove or at least conservatory plants, few people had the facilities in which to keep them and the plants themselves were hugely expensive.

It was the activities of the East India Company in Canton in their search for the tea plant *Camellia sinensis* that first brought ornamental camellias to the attention of the West. These exotic plants were brought home by the East India Company's sea captains and it was these few early imports that started the great camellia love affair of the nineteenth century.

First came the lovely pure white double 'Alba Plena' in 1792, closely followed by 'Variegata' introduced by Captain Corner for Mr. J Slater. The early years of the new century saw 'Grenville's Double Red', introduced by him in 1801. 'Incarnata' followed in 1806, imported from China for Sir Abraham and Lady Amelia Hume, of Wormleybury, Hertfordshire, and renamed 'Lady Hume's Blush' from a faint pink tinge between its petals. In 1816 and 1819, two sea captains imported varieties that were to assure them a place in history: Captain Welbank brought back 'Welbankiana' in 1816: it bloomed at Mr Turner's home, Rook's Nest Place in Surrey in 1819. The next year Captain Richard Rawes brought back the first garden variety reticulata 'Captain Rawes' which he gave to his brother-in-law Thomas Cary Palmer. It flowered in his conservatory in Bromley in Kent in 1826. →

These early camellias were originally imported for private enthusiasts but soon the nurseries of the day began to acquire imports for themselves. *Camellia japonica flore plena simplice* 'Single White' was said to have been introduced by nurseryman Mr. Rollisson *"or by a Lady who gave it him"*. *Flore pleno atrorubens* was introduced by nurserymen Loddiges & Sons in 1816 and 'Alba Plena Fimbriata' for nurseryman Colville in 1816.

C. Maliflora, like *C. reticulata* four years later, had been imported by Captain Rawes for Mr. Palmer, though it was soon distributed by a commercial nurseryman Mr. Lee. These and the other few varieties were to form the basis of the camellia nursery industry in England. In 1819 William Curtis's *Botanical Magazine* listed 29 different varieties. By 1831, nurseryman Alfred Chandler, in his publication *'Illustrations and descriptions of the plants which compose the natural order Camelliæ: and of the varieties of Camellia japonica cultivated in the gardens of Great Britain'* records details of forty different species and varieties including sixteen imports from China and nineteen English bred varieties. In some cases, we know a little about the parentage, 'Althaeiflora' is a chance seedling of Amenoniflora', raised in 1819 and which first bloomed in 1825. Chandler records seven new varieties that were all 'Amenoniflora' seedlings. This phrase, *a chance seedling*, is repeated often in the 19th century Verschaffelt catalogues when describing new introductions. Not all was left to chance, however, and new varieties were produced by the deliberate crossing of particular varieties in an attempt to incorporate desired characteristics.

By the 1860s the number of varieties had increased to several thousand: one nurseryman alone, William Bull, stocked over three hundred different cultivars.

So how was this huge increase achieved? The production of seedlings either by chance or deliberate crossing would have accounted for a great many, but the process is slow. The grex of seedlings that Alfred Chandler obtained from 'Amenoniflora' in 1819 took six years to flower and, only once flowering has taken place, could the selection and propagating process begin.

There is another way in which new varieties are produced and that is through sports. Before I began my association with camellias, I understood the verb 'to sport' as meaning to make playful if perhaps rather derisive mockery of someone, and I have since had no reason to change my mind. The botanical interpretation is, however, to produce mutations. Playful and good-humoured sporting might sound, but to the uninitiated trying to identify camellias, it is alarming. There is, however, a really positive side to this. Sports are one of the most important ways in which new varieties are produced.

The colour range of camellias is limited to shades of white through to red, apart from the recently discovered yellow *C. nitidissima*. What gives the flowers their enormous variety is the form of the bloom itself, single, peony, anemone or double, together with the way in which colours are distributed as stripes, streaks, blotches, flakes and borders.

Colour distribution has two recognised causes. The first and most important in this context is genetic variegation.

Over the years, camellias have been crossed, back-crossed and re-crossed and therefore contain a mixture of genetic material. Japonicas have a high propensity to mutate and these mutations can result in a plant that is composed of two or more genetically different tissues, known as a chimera. True natural sports usually come from chimeras.

In camellia chimeras, there are two different ways in which the different tissues are arranged. Sectorial chimeras are where tissues of different genetic constitution lie alongside each other; in cross section this would look like a piece of pie in a piechart. →

Sectorial chimera: schematic cross-section of camellia stem showing segments of different genetic material.

Buds arising from the red sector will produce flowers in accordance with that genetic material.

Buds that erupt from one particular segment produce flowers that are different from the main plant and those flowering shoots continue to produce those same flowers, every season.

An example of this is *Camellia japonica* 'Lavinia Maggi' and her sport 'Lavinia Maggi Rosea'.

Camellia japonica 'Lavinia Maggi', van Houtte 1858

Camellia japonica 'Lavinia Maggi Rosea', William Bull Catalogue 1867

Camellia japonica 'General Lamoricière' regularly produces a sport 'General Lamoricière Pink' whose colouration is the reverse of the normal flower. →

Camellia japonica 'General Lamoricière'
Guichard Soeurs Catalogue 1909

Camellia japonica 'General Lamoricière Pink'
Griffiths and Strothers 1954

In periclinal chimeras, the layers of different genetic tissue surround each other, in cross-section they would look like concentric circles. In shoots where the top layers are not complete, rather like a hand covered by a glove with holes in, buds that erupt can come from one or other layer of tissue, or they can come from areas where the tissues join, so that one layer might produce pink flowers, another layer white flowers and those produced from the junction of these layers may be bi-coloured.

The cause of these spontaneous mutations is thought to be transposones or jumping genes, mobile segments of DNA that can move from one chromosome to another causing mutations. The nearer to the growing tip or meristem that these mutations take place, the more likely it is that flower sports will be produced. The white or greenish white stripe so often seen in 19th century camellias is caused by mutation in this area of the shoot.

Camellia japonica 'Arciduchessa Augusta', van Houtte 1846, showing the distinctive white stripes.

The mixing of the genetic material can have some surprising results. The following photographs show a sport that occurred on *Camellia japonica* 'Mary Thomas (Heligan)' in 2007.

Camellia japonica 'Mary Thomas (Heligan)'

Sport from *Camellia japonica* 'Mary Thomas (Heligan)'

For this particular plant, the production of a sport seems to be a rare occurrence; I have not noticed any other unusual flowers. The same cannot be said for one of Heligan's other old camellias, known only as Camellia 26. This is an extraordinary camellia that regularly produces all manner of sports, flowers that are different in both colour and form. The American camellia 'Betty Sheffield' (Thomasville Nursery Catalogue 1951) is credited with at least twenty-six different sports, twenty-two of which are listed in the International Camellia Register and some of these sported varieties sport other forms!
None of the Camellia 26 sports has yet been stabilised but the number of sports produced is so prolific that it might, in the future, found a dynasty to rival that of 'Betty Sheffield'! →

The following photographs show a few of the sports produced in the last couple of years. These variations are caused by the random arrangement of the genetic material and in a plant like this, the genetic material is likely to be arranged in incomplete concentric layers. It seems that solid coloured flowers erupt from one set of genetic material and solid white flowers from another. Flowers that are a mixture of the two have come from junctions between these two. One of the problems in trying to propagate these flowers is that the shoots on which they appear are often unusually weak. Frequently they are very short or even show no sign of new growth at all. For this reason they are difficult to propagate. ➜

These forms have to be stabilised so that new varieties can be produced. The first problem, however, is to mark the desired flower forms. This needs to be done in such a way that the shoots can be recognised several months later, but without attracting undue interest from the public in the meantime. The first year I did this at Heligan, I tied small lengths of red ribbon to the shoots. I chose red because I thought the shoots would be easier to locate but then I overheard a visitor explaining to her friend that the ribbons were part of a religious ceremony! In a way she was quite right, I do take this camellia very seriously!

Colour is not the only characteristic that is valued in sports. One of the earliest recorded sports is 'Fimbriata', a sport of 'Alba Plena' imported from China in 1816 for Mr. Colville whose nursery was in the King's Road, Chelsea.

Notes from Loddige's *Botanical Cabinet* of 1826 describe it perfectly: *"There is an uncommon degree of delicacy and beauty in this flower. The original double white camellia is doubtless a most exquisite plant which scarcely anything can surpass, yet the one now before us, from the finely fringed edge of the petals, has a novel character peculiarly its own."* →

'Fimbriata' from an original painting by Mademoiselle G Fontaine, date 1840
Reproduced by courtesy of the RHS Lindley Library

These sports, interesting in themselves, add to the repertoire of camellias to propagate. They can also have a second value, that of helping to identify the variety of camellia on which they appear. This was so with a camellia that I had identified using the illustrations from the Verschaffelt catalogues as 'Auguste Delfosse', Verschaffelt 1855. I was not entirely happy with the identification, however, because I had come across plants supposedly of this variety that were somewhat different. (There is another variety 'Auguste Delfosse (Andre)' originating in France and known by the same name in the US.)

This camellia had proved hard to propagate and I had to resort to tying tiny cuttings onto pieces of pea stick to support the cuttings in the compost. Only one cutting rooted and, when it bloomed, the flowers were quite unlike those on the original plant. It was not until several years later that I realised that what I had inadvertently propagated was the recognised sport of 'Auguste Delfosse' and it was this that convinced me that my identification of the old camellia was correct.

How I came to propagate the sport I do not know since the old tree has shown no signs of sporting. The most likely explanation is that, in trying to propagate from a very small amount of new growth, I had damaged the genetic material close to the tip of the shoot and therefore encouraged the production of the sport.

Sports of Cam 35, *Camellia japonica* 'Auguste Delfosse'

Colour variegation in camellias is not always the result of the mixing of genetic material, it can also be the result of a viral infection, natural or deliberate. The origin of the natural virus is unknown; most likely it is one common to areas where the camellia is indigenous and spread by an equally indigenous insect vector. It seems that the insect vector did not make the journey to Europe and there are no known vectors spreading the virus. The virus is transmitted by grafting and continued by vegetative propagation.

The virus variegated camellias can also produce what are regarded as sports, for example 'Gloire de Nantes' produces the white-flaked variegation 'Gloire de Nantes Variegated'. This is regarded as a sport although some would argue that these sports are not produced by a rearrangement of genetic material, rather by the influence of environmental factors on the existing genetic material of the mother plant and are therefore forms of the same cultivar rather than distinct genetic entities. →

Camellia japonica 'Gloire de Nantes'
Guichard Soeurs Catalogue 1894

Camellia japonica 'Gloire de Nantes Variegated'
Vandebilt 1941

One of the real joys of this propensity of japonica varieties to sport is that it gives anyone the opportunity to raise a variety of their very own . . . .

Sporting does not happen only on old trees such as the ones I have used as examples in this text. Young plants can surprise you as well. Last year I came across *C. j.* ' Bonomiana' (van Houtte 1858) bearing a white sport (or perhaps form) and my prize to date is a young plant of *C. j.*'Hagomoro', (imported into Italy 1886) one whole branch of which bears a distinctive formal double.

I have not been able to find out so far if this is a recognised sport: if not, I have promised to name it for my mother!

Enys Gardens
St Gluvias, Near Penryn
by Barry Champion with photos by Tony Kent (except archive material)

Impressions of a gardener's visit.

Head Gardener at Trelissick Garden

It is said that the garden at Enys is the first ever to have received public notice, that is to say, the oldest recorded garden in Cornwall. So my visit was to be one of great anticipation. I was not to be disappointed.

The recorded history of the property begins with Robert de Enys who lived there during the reign of Edward I (1272 – 1307). The 1709 edition of Camden's Magna Britannia mentioned that Enys was noted for its fine gardens. It has a long illustrious past, but in more recent times has slowly slipped into a sleepy garden of great charm.

This process is not dissimilar to that of a lot of Cornish gardens in the 21st century. When two World Wars and a continued decline of gardeners' skill base plus the fact of the lack of financial investment, saw most gardens fall in standards of care and maintenance.

Through the forethought and vision of the late Professor G.L.Rogers, the then owner in 2002 a charity was formed, the Enys Trust, to secure the long term future of the gardens at Enys. The Trustees aims are to restore them to their former glory and also to make them more widely available to the public. Most members of the Cornwall Garden Society will recognise the difficult task which lies ahead for the Trust because of the commitment required from a financial, labour and management perspective in its preservation. This process will be one of gradual restoration trying to retain some of its 'lost' charm but raising the standards and content conducive to its listing in the English Heritage Register of Historic Gardens as a Grade II garden.

The visitor enters the property via the Enys Lodge to be greeted by a long linear parc which has mature deciduous trees and specimen conifers, unusually dominated by very large Turkey Oaks *(Quercus cerris)*. Two main points of interest are, respectively: on the left-hand side, a run of several hundred yards of Rhododendron 'Russellianum' (R.Cornish Red), a magnificent sight when in full bloom. Whilst, on the other, a superb view is afforded looking into the town of Falmouth. →

Passing over the second cattle grid, you now enter the pleasure grounds proper and the visitor can immediately see the contrasts: one of neglect and one of great charm. It is this single fact that the trustees have to deal with in their restoration programme, standards are being improved whilst retaining some of its 'lost' charm. In this part of the garden you can see some mature and new plantings dominated, unfortunately, by *Rhododendron ponticum* and *Prunus lauroceraceus*, a theme continued throughout the garden. The onslaught of these quite invasive plants has had, singularly, the most negative effect on the overall plant collection. Continuing down the rather neglected drive to the grass car-park, one can see the woodland plantings which protect the garden from the more severe weather conditions which we still get in Cornwall. Free from the constraints of the motor car, we can explore at our leisure. We approach the rear of the mansion, passing the Mowhay and the farm buildings to view the unusual (in Cornwall) clock tower. The design of which is very 'Italian'. Possibly the design brought back from the grand tour, by a previous owner. Walking to the front of the mansion, one passes under a fine *Fagus sylvatica* 'Asplenifolia' (fern leaved Beech) and, towards the right, a magnificent *Acer platanoides* 'Schwedleri' standing at 18 metres, one of the champion trees in the garden.

The Italianate Clock Tower

The Parkland from the south front of the mansion

The Pleasure Grounds

The outline of the formal garden on the south front can still be seen with probably the largest *Cleyera japonica* 'Tricolor' in Cornwall. But what sets this off as the most exquisite vista on the whole estate is the quite magnificent 'English' parkland. This rolling demesne is punctuated by fine specimen trees culminating with natural stands of native woodland which secures this enchanting scene from any outside influence.

Turning left and descending a short flight of steps, we enter the pleasure grounds proper. This area, which runs down to the 'productive' kitchen garden, would be described as typically Cornish, with Rhododendron, Camellia and Magnolias dominating the plant collection. But the more discerning student of horticulture would identify outstanding examples of the Chilean laurel *(Laurelia sempervirens)* and another champion tree, the Mockernut Hickory *(Carya tomentosa)* standing 16 metres tall. Passing the Laurelia on the right hand side of the path we approach the equally outstanding *Osmanthus heterophyllus* 'Variegatus'. This too is the largest specimen in Britain (8 metres). Because of the layout of the pleasure grounds, there is no formal recommended route so, as a visitor, you can discover at your ease, the delights of the garden in a very relaxed manner. →

It might well be appropriate at this stage to suggest to the visitor that their eye might be attracted to the loftier plants which dominate:
There are some quite spectacular trees, of which the following are of note: Turkey and Lucombe Oaks, both well over 30 metres tall. Two Podocarpus: *P. salignus* and *P. totara*, the latter was the tallest in the country but, although it lost its leader in the 1990 storm, it still remains an outstanding tree. Both the male and female forms of *Araucaria araucaria* (Monkey Puzzle) and, continuing the conifer theme, a magnificent *Cryptomeria japonica* var. *sinensis*. The most unusual, if not unique plant, is *Fagus sylvatica f. purpurea*: this is a grafted plant at about 3 metres and, below the graft, two side branches have been left to grow on. Both these side branches are the size of trees in their own right and it has been suggested that this was an apprentice piece. It would seem that the green and purple forms growing on the same tree to such a majestic size must be quite a feature in any garden. Another outstanding plant, north-east of the house is a 22 metre high *Ginkgo biloba*, reputedly a female form. Quite near this Maidenhair tree is the Gardener's Cottage where refreshments are served, delicious home made cakes and scones. Well worth the entry fee, just to sample Sue's wonderful home cooking!

Continuing our walk north through the garden, one is suddenly presented with a most wonderful view down to the water garden. A series of ponds which, in the 17th Century, were described as canals.
Unfortunately this area has restricted access at this time, but its beauty can be appreciated from the upper path. A view, flanked by a small collection of Acers, with what is quite an unusual feature in our Cornish gardens: a 'Laurel Lawn'. This 'lawn' disguises and shields a footpath which would otherwise interrupt one's view of the pond. Tree ferns and bamboos enhance the beauty of this most restful and peaceful of scenes. It may be prudent at this time to mention the remains of a water wheel and ram pump, both in quite good condition, placed beside the ponds to elevate water, for domestic purposes, to the mansion. It never ceases to amaze me how inventive our predecessors were in using nature rather than fossil fuels to complete what would, today, be a complicated process. →

The Enys water-wheel and ram pump

Bluebells in Parc Lye

A few paces on and the visitor alights, in mid April/May, on probably the finest asset of Enys's many delights, the expansive display of bluebells in what is known as 'Parc Lye'. This area, covering several acres, is believed to have been undisturbed since ancient times and is unsurpassed in any other Cornish garden.

The Summerhouse

Bearing right towards the 'Kitchen Garden' one discovers the 'Broad Walk', a wide walk which culminates in a summer house which seems in terminal decline. The walk itself is flanked by an eclectic collection of plants including Rhododendron, Camellia, Halesia and a banana, *Musa basjoo*. One of the most interesting features along the walk is a collection of minerals erroneously described as a rockery. This is, without doubt, an important part of the history of the garden, as the family were important mine owners in the county.

Two other features which should be mentioned are:

Firstly, The 12th Century Cornish Cross introduced to the garden in 1848 by John Samuel Enys, which was acquired from the vicar of Sancreed in payment for 'a cart load of things'. No record has survived of what those goods were, but I am sure they were value-for-money for such an important piece of Cornish history.

Secondly, right beside the Cross is a granite cyder press with an engraved date of 1796. Cyder presses are not unusual, but this one is dated, which is a very rare occurrence. →

The Enys 12th century Cornish cross

On the south side of the 'Kitchen Garden' is the Flower Garden which, at the present time, is being restored by the small and dedicated garden team, led by Mr Martin Mattock.

Upon entering, you are immediately confronted by the very beautiful *Lagarstrobus franklinii* (the Huon Pine), not grown extensively in Cornwall.

The flower beds are clearly defined by large spar stones in a very attractive manner.

These beds contain some trees, shrubs and mainly herbaceous subjects grown in a quite haphazard, but pleasing way.

The walls of a lean-to glass house are to be seen with the thermo-siphon heating system still in situ.

At the bottom of the 'Flower Garden' is the 'Colonels Garden', a small walled enclosure which is at the present time being developed with a scented theme.

The dominant feature is the Italianate Gateway which leads to the wilderness. Although a small space, it does have a charm all to itself and when the existing planting matures, it will be a delightful resting place for the relief of the stresses and strains of modern life. →

The fern seat in the Flower Garden

Part of the Kitchen Garden pre 1914

The 'Kitchen Garden' which, at present, is not open to the public, contains several interesting features, some of which are historically very important. The delightful small building takes centre stage, being used as a toolshed, cribroom and Head Gardener's office. The equipment contained therein suggest that the garden staff, 100 years ago, just walked away, leaving everything in situ. On the east wall can clearly be seen, two tall pavilions which are evident on the Borlaise print of 1758, both are slightly altered, one to an apple store and the other, into a desirable Head Gardener's cottage. Throughout the walled garden, evidence of its former use i.e. standing-out frames, bases of former glass houses, dipping pond, and a remarkable, and still in good condition, saddle-back boiler which heated all the greenhouses via a thermo-syphon system.

It is quite impossible to relay to the reader all the history and charms of such a romantic garden, suffice to say that Enys is one of the most important of all our beautiful Cornish gardens. Its long history, its relationship with the surrounding countryside, the biodiversity contained within the estate and, of course, in the past, the very extensive plant collection.

In 1909, J.D.Enys produced a list of 'Trees, Shrubs and Plants' growing at Enys, of over 1000 taxon, he in fact became a much travelled plant collector. His speciality of New Zealand flora, instrumental in introducing the Chatham Island Forget-me-not, *Mysiotidium hortensia* into this country. Whilst in New Zealand, he established a sheep station and built a house, albeit basic, and called it Trelissick, after his grandfather's estate in Feock. (Hence my interest in the Enys garden). Time has greatly reduced the range of plants grown and most of the physical features need tender loving care, a task which the Trustees and garden staff are enthusiastically putting all their energies into achieving.

If any reader would be interested in offering their individual skills as a volunteer, please contact me on 01872 870750. A whole range of skills are required. Please give me a ring to discuss.
To put into words a written description of such an atmospheric and magical garden is practically impossible, suffice to say that a visit to Enys would be the only way to experience the spirituality of this, the most beautiful of Cornish gardens.

Enys Opening times:
Tues & Thurs afternoons at 2.00
1st Sunday of the month at 2.00 1st April – 1st October
Group guided tours 01872 870750

"Becoming a Botanist"
by Keith Spurgin
Keith is a former BSBI recorder for West Cornwall

Western Ramping-fumitory
Photo Keith Spurgin

> *'The fresh unchristened things appear*
> *Leaf spathe and stem*
> *With crumbs of earth clinging to them*
> *To show the way they came;*
> *But no flower yet to know their name...'*

Andrew Young was a nature poet whose gems include Swallows, Dead Mole and the delightfully evocative Sudden Thaw, quoted (and possibly mis-quoted) above.

Word-pictures drawn by his pen included those of swallows, 'jugglers with their own bodies in the air' and a single green spear 'stabbing a dead leaf from below' to banish winter. Not that anything so violent is usually needed in Cornwall, where winter has been described as 'more of a languid spring'. Young came here to hunt for rare plants, a self-confessed 'botanophile', what birders would call a 'twitcher'; following his passion as it led him along cliff paths and across wet moors. What did he make of our Cornish gardens? – So frequently the recipient of unconsidered treasures, sometimes even the very rarities he sought with such easy pleasure.

It may be hard to turn from what we call nature to our role as gardener, which changes day by day from supervisor to labourer, and sometimes (rarely?) even to a contented owner, basking in a visitor's praise; because one of the feelings associated with following this gentle occupation of ours is, surprisingly, guilt! Did you get those Sweet Peas sown in November? Are your potatoes chitted? And did you stop ogling that catalogue long enough to actually order next season's seeds? Another layer of guilt is heaped on you by all the advice spawned by everything from encyclopaedias to calendars, telling you when to lift this or divide that. And those T.V. gardeners! Don't they know we can see the teams of workers toiling in the background while they mark out a few perfectly straight rows; or, worse, plant the Sweet Peas they germinated in November?

Like an unturned compost heap these layers accumulate until you begin to wonder if you should after all move to somewhere with a smaller garden....... For those nodding in even slight agreement with these rather ironic remarks, I'm pleased to be able to suggest a remedy:

The first step is to take up an interest in Botany – not more unrequited labour, you might protest – do you really want to know the difference between Sun Spurge and Petty Spurge? They're both pests, poisonous and possessed of unlimited seed banks. And surely we've had enough of a problem remembering the Tree-spurge *Euphorbia mellifera* or Mediterranean Spurge *E. characias*, which we might actually want to grow.

Why bother with mere 'weeds'? For several very good reasons, I say. The *pleasure* of being able to point out *Veronica hederifolia* to the 'Garden Inspectors' (more of which anon) must make up for a little study. Especially when the most seasoned of them, the Hardy Plant Specialist, for instance, may look slightly puzzled before pronouncing '*That's* a weed'. To which you will then have full authority to reply 'I know. I'm *studying* them. There are two subspecies you know', bearing in mind that 'studying' clearly includes 'glancing at occasionally from your deckchair while doing the crossword'.

Yes, Ivy-leaved Speedwell may live up to its name in your garden, sprouting its legions of seedlings with their small blue flowers, and hairy, lobed leaves, but you may find it interesting to compare with Germander Speedwell *V. chamaedrys*, its country cousin, which has distinctive stems, hairy on two opposite sides and smooth on the other two. When you then realise that about a dozen Speedwell species have been recorded in Cornwall, you might even want to name some more of them.

Or if, like a farmer, you're looking for a return, you might invest a moment or two identifying Cornsalad *Valerianella*, now sold in supermarkets, but almost certainly in a garden near you. It was once consumed in quantity under the name of Lamb's Lettuce and (in my garden) is routinely picked along with 'human' lettuce. Its minute blue flowers are distinctive but for accurate identification you need to have ripe seeds.

These days it will probably be Keel-fruited Cornsalad *V. carinata*; the others are mostly arable associates, now decreasing under pressure from intensive agriculture. This comes in handy when your Wholefood Expert Garden Inspector is chatting to you about organic varieties. You can casually offer them a plant or two and, even if they say 'Ah, Cornsalad!' you can say 'Yes, but which species?' →

If this seems a small return for the time invested, you can plunge straight into the genus *Geranium*, a delight to behold and interesting to Cornish botanists who have most of the dozen or so wild species to admire. As an added spur to Becoming a Botanist you can refer your Hybrid Specialist to *Geranium* x *oxoniense*. This is the cross between Pencilled Crane's-bill *G. versicolor* and French Crane's-bill *G. endressii*. A 'good idea at the time' it has become a garden centre cliché, with some varieties both gaudy and competitive. 'Pencilled' is a beautiful species, sometimes found on shaded banks, especially in West Cornwall while 'French' is a rare casual. The hybrid 'escapes' occasionally (or is thrown out more likely) and is recorded occasionally outside its garden habitats. For good measure you can refer to the variety *thurstonii*, which has oddly inrolled petals. You can even show your energy efficiency credentials by failing to weed out Herb-robert *G. robertianum* from its paving cracks and borders or allowing Dove's-foot Crane's-bill *G. molle* to flourish in your lawn.

The Garden Inspectors can of course be totally benign, ranging as they do from the Mastermind contestant who knows every moss, lichen and fungus to your neighbour who is secretly wondering if you're ever going to offer a cup of tea. Sooner or later they depart, and you are left to experiment further with the 'hands-off' method. Suddenly that patch you were going to dig over can be left to its own devices.

In the first year there will probably be Willowherb *Epilobium* species to decipher. Their floating seeds emulate the willows after which they are named and again about a dozen species have been recorded in Cornwall.

Bramble seedlings mark beds and borders near bird perches, and if left long enough may give you a fine bush of 'Himalayan Giant', the cultivated Blackberry, free of charge. Yes it's true that you might also have one of the hundred or so other Cornish species but this could be a bonus! Most of the fruit of these wild types is quite palatable and you can also impress the Mastermind by referring to the *three hundred plus* species recorded for the British Isles. Even serious botanists run in terror from the thorny genus *Rubus* so the chances are you'll be on safe ground.

Now it may just happen that you have already Become a Botanist, in which case you'll know that you're probably more likely to find Petty Spurge than Sun Spurge, the latter usually being more of an arable species. Both have a penchant for disturbed ground, which brings me to another group that even some serious botanists may hesitate before identifying. These are the fumitories, noted camp-followers and easy enough to recognise as a group, with their miniature spires of 20 or so cylindrical flowers, rarely more than half-an-inch (12mm) long and pale, often pinkish coloured, tinged red or dark purple at the tip. They seed quickly, usually before you notice them, a good survival technique; another is the viability of seeds, which can run into decades, like the poppies and crucifers.

Their bitter juice, nature's slug-repellent, was once prized by our forebears as a remedy for eye disorders but now they are 'just weeds'? Or are they? Every other year it seems a journalist discovers that Feverfew *Tanacetum parthenium* is a cure for migraine; and Nettle soup is an old standby in alternative recipe books (delicious, by the way). Perhaps the fumitories are poised for a comeback, but aren't we still looking at our uninvited guests for what we can get out of them? As wild food or a cure for something, instead of enjoying them for their own sake?

A 'x10' hand lens brings a whole new world into focus and is the astronomer's telescope of the galaxy in miniature that awaits inspection in your garden.

One day I noticed that a bee was busy cutting a hole in the calyx of a Red Campion *Silene dioica* (which has a resident's permit in our garden), apparently to get quick access to nectar at the base of the flower-tube. Later I watched as an ant climbed the stem and robbed nectar from this ready-made hole in the wall. I've never seen a pollinator at work on a Fumitory, but early in the morning you can see the beautiful display of droplets at the tips of the leaf-lobes, as the plants 'guttate', more food for ants.

To the sheer pleasure of observation you can add that of knowing that Cornwall has become something of a fumitory-factory. We have all the large-flowered species recorded for the British Isles plus Common Fumitory *Fumaria officinalis*, which makes seven altogether. Of these one is endemic (in the sense of 'only native in') the British Isles, one is endemic to Cornwall and Scilly, and one an extremely rare colonist in Southern England. Fumitories have a special penchant for newly-built Cornish hedges and could turn up on any patch of disturbed ground near you.

An added incentive to the plant-hunter is the appearance of several fumitories on the Red Data List.

Begun in 1977, this is the definitive catalogue of rare and threatened species in the British Isles. Of our Cornish plants, international responsibility exists for White Ramping-fumitory and Western Ramping-fumitory is nationally scarce. →

White-ramping fumitory
Photo Keith Spurgin

Purple Ramping-fumitory is both nationally scarce and subject to international responsibility. Common Ramping-fumitory and Martin's Ramping-fumitory are on the *Waiting List*. This designation is a holdall for plants about which there is uncertainty as to their status or identity. Is 'Martin's' a very rare native or a series of chance introductions? And the extent to which two subspecies of 'Common' exist in the British Isles (including, if at all) needs to be worked out. After 400 years during which our flora has been exhaustively examined, it is good to know that challenges still exist.

Still you may find the challenge posed by the fumitories a little too much. After all, wasn't I promising a panacea for all that guilt? Trying to run down plants from books can begin to resemble thumbing through a medical dictionary. After a while you begin to imagine that every single entry is what you have. You carefully put your book away - often with a scrap of the unidentified species pressed inside it. Soon enough the bittercresses *Cardamine* species, busy little seeders, will arrive without an invitation to your garden party. Wavy Bitter-cress, taller, bulkier, with a zig-zag stem, is more likely to be seen in damp situations in the wild; whereas Hairy Bitter-cress is smaller and straighter. One problem with plant identification is the reliance we place on names. You just can't separate these two on whether or not one is hairy and one smooth. Diminutive relatives of the mighty Mustards and Cabbages, which we actually want, they have tough seeds that last long. Another string to their bow is the propulsive mechanism that rolls up like a runaway blind, spilling the seed yards from the parent plant. Annual Meadow-grass *Poa annua*, a cosmopolitan weed, will be everywhere from plant pots to chimney pots and as for Bindweed *Calystegia sepium*...! This survives by the very weakness of its roots. If only they wouldn't break when you pulled them, allowing whole new systems to develop seemingly overnight. As for Couch-grass *Elytrigia repens*, which in Cornwall was once called 'Stroil', it's another born survivor. I have found the white, sharp-pointed roots piercing Bluebell bulbs.

And it's no good being fatalistic and considering that after all we introduced a lot of these enemies of ease. Take Winter Heliotrope *Petasites fragrans*, its round leaves and dingy pink but vanilla-scented flowers covering hedgebanks, verges and neglected garden corners for all the world as if it was always here. But the Daisy relative that used to go by the name of 'Rat-plant' in Cornwall arrived, it is said, with a fully completed travel permit. Apparently it was grown for the sole purpose of supporting the trade in Sweet Violets *Viola odorata*, those big round leaves being just what was wanted to wrap around the posies to keep them fresh. And to bind them? Well, bindweed of course. Another honoured guest that has outlived its welcome is Japanese Knotweed *Fallopia japonica*. Originally imported for ground cover in large estates it is now the subject of strict control measures.

At the other end of the scale of social acceptability lies Weasel's-snout *Misopates orontium*, a close relative of our friend the Snapdragon, itself a prodigious self-seeder.

Weasel's-snout is becoming scarcer in our islands generally but hangs on in Cornwall, having a particular niche in allotments, where its little purple-pink, pouched flowers seem to be tolerated despite contributing nothing but their innocent beauty.

An even more acceptable species is the daisy-like Mexican Fleabane *Erigeron karvinskianus*. Crossing the Atlantic, it turned up at St. Peter Port, Guernsey in 1870, spreading onto the mainland soon afterwards and now a feature of walls and dry ground, especially in Cornwall. You see it particularly in coastal situations, separated from the familiar Daisy *Bellis perennis* (partly) by having leaves up the stem instead of in a rosette.

Another relatively recent addition to our flora is that miniature of dampish, shady situations in our gardens, Mind-your-own-business *Soleirolia soleirolii*. Arriving from the islands of the west Mediterranean, its minute round leaves grow by the million to form a green cloak over banks, bare ground and stonework. A resident of Carbis Bay told me that his lawn was 'infested' with it. So he wrote to a firm of horticulturalists and asked if they could identify it from a photo he had taken. No, alas. But they were able to tell him that they sold it!

Many escapes and introductions set up shop, make a quick killing then themselves die back, exemplifying true boom and bust behaviour. In Truro every few years there is a splurge of some hanging-basket speciality. Recently both *Polygonum capitata*, a small plant with heavily-marked leaves and small round heads, and a *Mimulus* of complex parentage brightened our streets before virtually disappearing again. In our greenhouses and gardens there are longer-term success stories like Procumbent Yellow-sorrel *Oxalis corniculata*. A small plant with clover-like leaves and pods full of seed, its weediness has been described as 'pernicious'.

More exotic passengers stow away in consignments of seeds. Those you buy from stores and garden centres are usually well-screened and nicely packaged but there are benefits from getting a twist of brown paper from a friend or a parcel of seed varieties from a non-commercial source. This year we had *Aster divaricatus* and a completely unknown Wood-sorrel *Oxalis* as adventives. If you want to explore this option you can join organisations like the Organic Garden (formerly the Henry Doubleday Research Association) or the South London Botanical Institute. Benefits include receiving seeds of often rare varieties that can no longer be sold because of licensing strictures.

Did I mention guilt? Now we're worrying about saving varieties like the famous Brighstone Pea, one that has survived thanks to a shipwreck on the Isle of Wight and its distribution to enthusiasts. A bit off the track when we're supposed to be enjoying our weeds. For surely our garden is the place to relax, not to worry about the fate of the planet? Well remember that lovely Old English word 'fallow', with its delightful connotations of doing not very much; perhaps Being a Botanist; or just watching Andrew Young's swallows.

Here's Food for Thought

DIARY OF THE COTSWOLDS SUMMER TOUR 5TH – 9TH AUGUST 2007

Words + photos by John Mann   Past President of the CGS

Sunday 5th

The Society's Summer tour of gardens in the Cotswold area started, unusually, on a Sunday. The reason was to avoid the busy time in late week at our hotel of choice, Three Ways House in Mickleton. It is the home of the Pudding Club, where nostalgia for filling puddings served with lashings of custard can be fully indulged. Our party had a modified menu on one evening; modified on account of those with dietary restriction, but one member still managed eight helpings. Lord Randall's pudding topped the poll, a steamed pudding with apricots and marmalade and its popularity was reflected in a shortage of the latter at breakfast the following morning.

A break in the journey was made at a small garden and nursery at the foot of the Mendip Hills, Mill Cottage Plants, near the village of Wookey. Sally Gregson has developed the two acre garden over the past 16 years around the river Axe which flows through the garden and under the house. A deck over the water provided a pleasant sitting spot to enjoy a cup of tea whilst looking down into a small secret garden and bog area. Behind the house, mixed borders of shrubs, perennials and grasses surrounded a lawn. Gravel paths led one to a secluded sitting spot via a pergola. On the tree-shaded river bank were small breaks in the cover where Damsel flies flashed their brilliance. The herbaceous planting contrasted pale colours and grasses with a hot border with dark foliage acting as a foil for the brighter colours. A gravel area catering for drought resistant plants made up a cosmopolitan array to delight the visitors.

Immediately, and much to the dismay of our new coach driver, the propensity of our members for retail therapy was indulged. Tall plants of *Veronicastrium virginicum* 'Fascination', Dierama, dark red gladiolus and *Iris siberica* vied for space on the coach with lower growing Geraniums and unusual forms of *Hydrangea serrata*.

Monday 6th

The garden of Hidcote Manor lies only a short walk from the hotel at Mickleton and many of our group took its advantage to shake down the cooked breakfast. The lame and the lazy arrived by coach at the same time. So much has been written about Lawrence Johnston and Hidcote which makes difficult a description of the garden with which one is so familiar, both by writings, previous visits and from the vignette presented by Chris Beardshaw at Chelsea Flower Show. This account then will be restricted to additions to most people's impressions of the garden.

Hidcote Manor

Monday 6th

Re-routing the entry to the garden, immediately introduces you to the borders with exuberant plantings of shrub roses and herbaceous plants. Much less of the south face of the house now appears visible and the cool walk beneath the Cedar of Lebanon was particularly inviting. The red borders, always popular, were holding up very well.

Hemerocallis fulva 'Flore Pleno'

After the heavy rain the roses were looking fine with Dahlias and Cannas, both with dark foliage. Cordylines adding texture, dark plumes of Buddleia 'Royal Red' attracting the insects but perhaps on this occasion *Hemerocallis fulva 'Flore Pleno'* stealing the show. By the steps leading to the pavilions the dark purple hoods of Aconitum 'Sparks Variety' were attracting much attention.

The Red Border

With adequate time to take one's ease in the garden, one was able to explore more closely the hidden corners and noting *Veratrum album* with giant white flower spikes, pink lilies and Thalictrum. Here a volunteer was attempting to capture the bright red lily beetles which quickly drop when disturbed then lie still on their backs, the brown underparts invisible in the woodland mulch. Perhaps a portable vacuum may be the answer.

Aconitum 'Sparks Variety'

The National Trust are to be congratulated for introducing the Plant House where a long-disintegrated structure had previously existed. During the warmer months it remains open fronted, becoming a glass house for the growing of tender species in the cooler periods. With a pool and colourful bedding in front, the whole becomes a very attractive feature. The old rose walk, behind, features modern planting of perennial and biennial plants.

Veratrum album

Thalictrum dipterocarpum

Good form of Eryngium made effective combination with a pink Phlox. The old favourite enclosures are still there with suitable plant rejuvenation, the introduction of new and improved forms as well as retaining the spirit of the historical plantings. Set on high ground with views across grazing sheep toward the Vale of Evesham, the garden still affords a refreshing visit for the garden lover and the plantsman alike. →

Monday 6th

Because of the proximity of the village of Badsey, a poll revealed that a short late afternoon trip to Bob Brown's Cotswold Garden Flowers was preferred to taking one's ease before the evening's activities. In spite of standing water in the surrounding fields, our brave coach driver took us all the way down the narrow track. We were rewarded by a warm welcome and a mass of colour in the trial beds. Considered intent and impulse buying were both heavily indulged, the huge range on view can rarely be found elsewhere and the hardest resolve to resist was easily overcome. Varieties of Helenium, Hemerocallis, Kniphofia and late flowering summer bulbs were easily identified being carried from the sales area along with several of the "Plant of the Year" from Chelsea, as identified by TV pundits, *Mathiasella bupleuroides* 'Green Dream'.

If that were not enough for one day, we returned in the early evening to the neighbouring property of Kiftsgate for both a stroll through the garden and a glass of Pimms on the terrace served by one of the proprietors of our hotel accompanied by his daughter.

The house stands on the edge of the escarpment overlooking the Vale of Evesham and the view in the haze of evening with gathering storm clouds was quite impressive. Equally, the view directly downward through the pine trees to the pool and lower garden with a Mediterranean feel tempts one to ignore the messages sent from weary knees.

Pimms at Kiftsgate

The impressive neo-classical frontage is home to immense climbers and the terraced gardens are richly planted and colourful. Three generations of garden makers and plant collectors make this a Mecca for plantsmen. Here one sees not just good plant selections but inspired associations.

The terrace immediately in front of the house in the form of four squares contained many red Roses and Fuschias, hardy Geraniums and Penstemons, Lilies and Gladioli, Honeysuckles and Clematis.

Pool and Lower Garden

At the side of the house, the sunken White garden is just amazing. Height is given by Eucryphia 'Nymansay', Viburnums and Philadelphus and two unusual Deutzias, *D. monbegii* and *D. sechuenensis* 'Corymbiflora'. Forms of *Hydrangea arborescens* and *H. paniculata* dominated the other shrubby surrounds. The small terraced beds teemed with small plants and sub shrubs with white flowers and/or silver foliage and additionally with the use of pots and containers.

A walk down the rose borders edged with arcure trained apples left one hankering for more roses in our own gardens, not always achievable in our damp climate. The boundary forest trees here are host to the massive growth of *Rosa filipes* 'Kiftsgate' whose display was largely finished.

Herbaceous bank with terrace beyond

A clair-voyée has been cut into the Yew hedge at the end of this border and gives a fascinating glimpse into a new pool. Strictly formal and modern in concept within tall Yew hedges it has paved edges set in grass and a rectangular island reached by large stepping stones.

At the far end a row of fountain heads resembling Anthurium leaves on tall stalks at different levels, each released a trickle of water according to some hidden programme. Much amusement was occasioned by some who had a theory that the water was released in response to triggering a sensor on the stepping stones.

The rain held off just long enough to allow a good study of the garden and an enjoyable Pimms before the heavens opened and we had to make a hasty retreat to our coach. This proved to be the only real curtailment to our programme, which was indeed fortunate considering the weather that had preceded the tour. →

Water Garden

48   THE CORNISH GARDEN

Tuesday 7th

We were dramatically reminded of that on the following morning as our route took us across the flood plains of both the Avon and the Severn. Here the flood levels were clearly indicated by deposits of detritus and damage to fences. The human misery could only be imagined where the high water mark was plainly seen on the walls of shops and houses in some of the villages we passed through and the depressing sight of skips containing carpets and furniture.

Our destination was Stockton Bury Farm near Leominster and a great favourite of the writer. The garden has grown up around the working farm buildings and farming activities still taking place involving cattle and sheep right in its centre. The owner, Raymond Treasure, the nephew of the late John Treasure of Burford Court and founder of Treasures of Tetbury, is a talented artist. Evidence of his artistry abounds in his choice of plants and colour schemes, landscaping and placement of artefacts, decoration and sympathetic restoration of the buildings and extending to the imaginative menu in the newly restored tithe barn restaurant.

One enters the garden through the Cider Press. Here there is a small plant sales area, selling unusual plants propagated from some of those growing in the garden. Even this area is made attractive by the addition of a small pool and rill. My favourite area comes next, sandwiched between two ancient buildings, stepping down from either of two approaches to curving borders with an amazing use of colour and texture. The background contains the pre-Reformation Pigeon House from a time when the farm was the property of the monks of Leominster Priory. Green, yellow and variegated foliage provides a foil for herbaceous planting including Helenium, Hemerocallis and exceptionally blue Eryngiums.

Stockton Bury Farm House

Behind the house lies a mainly Spring garden with a delightful little summer house with walls decorated with flower paintings. The tidy and decorative vegetable garden, glasshouses and Iris garden border the long walk on one side. On the other a series of compartments with abundant and colourful planting in a variety of styles. Autumn flowering Gentians beside a trickling rock pool, the tissue paper flowers of Romneya lighting up a shady corner, the careful placing of pots and watering cans brought smiles of wonderment.

A large area of island beds with mixed planting revealed many unusual treasures. *Gleditisia triacanthos* 'Ruby Lace' was used to effect and *Mahonia gracillipes* with small red flowers caught the eye.

Paddock Garden

I especially liked the pillar garden. Here sandstone obelisks stood in double borders viewed through wrought iron gates. The planting was delightfully light yet containing many hot colours. Crocosmia, Helenium, Dahlia, Rudbeckia, orange lilies and Eschscholzia contrasting with masses of pale blue Nepeta gave an effect reminiscent of a flowering meadow.

Pillar Garden

The Dingle, developed from a wet hollow to celebrate the new millennium, has a trickling meandering stream with interconnecting pools. It is lavishly planted with moisture loving plants especially Iris and is a suitable climax to the walk through the garden. A route through the hidden grotto starts the return journey which can still find surprises. →

The Dingle

Tuesday 7th

Tuesday afternoon took us on to Stone House Cottage Nurseries near Kidderminster, where a garden to compliment the nursery business has been created in an old walled garden. To the walls have been added towers and follies and arches to further accommodate the climbing plants which are the particular strengths of the nursery. The central area has crossing double herbaceous borders with good showing from Phlox, Monarda, Agapanthus, Galega and Verbascum. Many shrubs provided the structure, and forms of Buddleia and Berberis, both with silver foliage, making a good contrast among the dominant greens. Nearer the house, low beds nurtured smaller subjects completing a very eclectic collection of plants. The nursery and garden compliment each other, the garden being almost the sole source of propagating material. As most were, in fact, propagated it was possible to seek out some fine treasures and a readiness to dig up bits made up for the chaos and untidiness of the sales area. The reasonable prices charged meant most of the party left with a smile, even if it was only for the state of the plumbing!

Stone House Cottage

Wednesday 8th

The following day, Wednesday, we were introduced to two very different gardens. One largely unchanged over the centuries and the other created in this century. The first, Rousham Park, near Bicester, was built for Sir Robert Dormer in 1635 and remains in the hands of the same family today. Our visit commenced with a tour of the interior by the lady of the house (and her dog). Much of the house dates back to the Jacobean era even to the musket holes in the front door, so that Sir Robert could train his musket on the advancing Parliamentarians. Fine paintings adorn the walls. The remodelling by William Kent begun in 1738 is largely as he left it, except for the windows. Later extensions retained the same style.

It is in the garden, however, that Kent's influence is most to be seen and his alterations to Bridgeman's previous plans are considered to be his best. The romantic journey through his Italianate landscape with terraces, statuary, ponds and cascades, temples and urns conjures up images of guests in glamorous costume strolling and gazing in wonder at the serpentine rill and taking the Long Walk, now a tunnel beneath overhanging branches of the fine trees - a marked contrast to the sight of some of our group in bright modern apparel taking their picnic on the bank of the River Cherwell. What, one wonders, was the purpose of the Cold Bath in so romantic a landscape?

Lion and Horse

I have never believed in fairies, so the sight of gentlemen with horns and goats trousers failed to excite, but the Dying Gladiator, and the Lion and Horse, both by Sheemakers, the latter in view from the house across the bowling green, are much more to my taste.

Pigeon House Garden

The walled garden behind the house, with its aged fruit trees, still retained some colour in its long border but the neighbouring Pigeon House Garden was exceptional. A lattice design of box edging complemented a brilliant display of roses. The old Pigeon House itself, dating from 1695, with its internal revolving ladder to reach the pigeon holes was still inhabited.

Although the motor car presence in front of the house brought one back to the present day, the Longhorn cattle in the paddock contrived to prolong the illusion. →

Longhorn cattle

Wednesday 8th

The stark contrast came as we transferred to the garden of Broughton Grange, near Banbury. A garden very new in style and concept and created around a walled area by Tom Stuart-Smith in 2001. The paved area within the walls has a tea room and pool and is dominated by a large Catalpa in full flower at the time of our visit. The entrance to the higher terrace has a well grown specimen of the newly discovered Wollemi Pine, one of four grown in the garden and noticeably larger at that time than that in the Tresco Abbey Garden.

The flowering terraces featured rounded and irregular patterns of box edging containing blocks of yellow and blue, together with a formal canal and cascade. All about was much silver foliage and fashionable use of grasses and Euphorbia.

Catalpa

Box edging

Flowering terrace

Modern planting style

View to future plantation

The view from this higher level showed a bare area of some 40 acres which was earmarked to become a tree plantation. Lower down, extensive planting had already commenced with a wide variety of broadleaved and conifer species.

An existing woodland area played host to a stumpery which was not proving successful and a peat garden where the peat block walls had lost their integrity during the earlier dry weather. Adjacent to the house was a more conventional herbaceous border and views to open countryside. The lower ground bordering the stream is to be developed as natural Wetland and water meadow. →

Thursday 9th

Thursday, the day of our return to Cornwall started early. Somehow the huge volume of plant purchases made during our tour had to be marshalled into reverse order of our leaving the coach.

Crates and carrier bags materialised from window sills and bathrooms and from shady corners of the hotel garden before breakfast so the coach could be packed. Somehow we also had to find room for our suitcases!

We broke our journey at Stow-on-the-Wold, divided into two groups and spent some time taking lunch and shopping while the others toured the Garden House, the home of Pam Schwerdt and Sybylle Kreuttzberger, one time head gardeners at Sissinghurst. Both had lectured to the Society and their plantsmanship was well known.

The tiny irregular shaped garden is testament to their skill and persistence. The entrance is already heavily shaded by a large tree and all the soil had to be brought to the site. A small sitting area and lawn with modest walls, so as not to overshadow the neighbours, the planting was rich and imginative.

The bright red seeds of *Paeonia mlokosewitschii* were noticed, tender plants in pots framed the doorway and climbers attached to the house appeared wherever there was support. Clematis 'Etoile Rose' was spectacular on a wire bower over the seating area.

Paeonia mlokosewitschii

The tall, aptly named Dahlia 'Magenta Star' with single flowers above very clean purple foliage stood out. It was on trial from Winchester Growers and promised to be a hit.

As well as forms of Cottage Garden favourites, some grasses were carefully placed and most effective. *Miscanthus nepalensis* was admired but most comment was reserved for the curly blond locks of *Stipa barbata*.

Dahlia 'Magenta Star'

As members said their thank-you's and filed out shaking their heads in disbelief, they were no doubt reflecting on how their own gardens could look with hard work.

At least they were halfway there ....

There was a bus-load of plants awaiting them!

Stipa barbata

Amazing gardens

Swashbuckling adventures

Locally-grown treats

Time travelling

Recharged batteries

Exotic plants

Looking for something different?

Wherever you are, you won't be far from somewhere special cared for by the National Trust. Visit **www.nationaltrust.org.uk/visitcornwall** or call **01208 74281** to see what the Trust has to offer you today.

THE NATIONAL TRUST

Fallen beech tree at Boconnoc

Boconnoc
The Future

by Anthony Fortescue of Boconnoc

photos Charles Francis

Trees are one of the glories of Boconnoc. From the ancient native trees in the Deer Park to the ornamental trees in the gardens they dominate the landscape.

Yet, in the past did we take them too much for granted?

There was a time when a sure sign of work going on in the woodlands was the wisp of smoke rising through the canopy of the trees. Fires would be kept going from day to day, the coals being damped down in the evening to be stirred back into life next morning with a prong.

Onto these pyres would be cast every bit of fallen timber and lop and top not needed as timber, for tool making or for firewood. Even fallen leaves would sometimes be raked up to leave a clean woodland floor behind the woodmen.

We only respected trees in the landscape when we could see that they were in rude health or when we thought they were growing into valuable timber. →

The sawbench

My interest in trees and timber increased when, in the 1970s, I started a business making fine furniture.
Although we used mainly imported timber, I was always on the look out for interesting ways of using timber from Boconnoc where we have our own sawmill. →

Crane to lift logs onto conveyor

The Sawmill complex

This is powered by a turbine driven by water collected in two header ponds. Installed in 1912 this alternative energy source was way ahead of its time. →

Drying shed for sawn timber

Drying shed for sawn timber

Racks of drying sawn timber

Our understanding of the environment has changed a great deal over the last two decades, and not just because of fears of global warming.

For most of us there has been a lot to learn, not least about the relationship between trees and the ecology of the countryside. I now see a tree not as a single organism growing independently of its surroundings but as part of an interdependent world of many species. It is during senescence and decline that a tree plays its most valuable role in the environment. Perhaps the most fascinating aspect of this is the dependence of trees on mychorrizal fungi and vice versa.
There are many forms of these fungus, the most exotic of these is the truffle which, sad to say, I have yet to find at Boconnoc!

Picture the canopy of a large tree and the weight of leaves within it in midsummer. Then consider the size of the root plate of a fallen tree. Even allowing for the smaller roots left in the ground how does the tree gather enough nutrients to support that canopy? The answer is, with difficulty. The most successful trees grow to the size that they do with the help of nutrients gathered from deep in the soil by mychorriza. The slender filaments of the fungus penetrate the living tissues of the tree for its own survival.

In their twilight world fungi are unable to photosynthesise and are therefore dependent on the tree to provide the carbon to sustain them. The mychorriza will sometimes be present at the birth of the tree; lurking in the seed such as an acorn. It helps the tree to establish itself and grow strong then, as the tree ages and dies it is slowly consumed by a whole variety of fungi. Sometimes the relationship gets out of balance and we have all experienced the loss of young trees from honey fungus.

Obviously we will go on harvesting timber from strong healthy trees at Boconnoc. Forestry is an important part of the economy of the estate. However, when we work through the woods we are now careful to leave the carcases of some older trees to enable this beneficial cycle to continue. Of course, the rotting away of dead trees, fallen branches and leaf litter all help to maintain the fertility of woodlands. To clear fell and remove all the material from a woodland compartment has the same effect as any form of monoculture; it steadily reduces the fertility of the soil. →

Fallen tree left in situ for wildlife

The action of fungus on the wood of a tree can also produce some interesting patterns which can be turned to good use in furniture making. The most obvious of this is "spalted" beech where the black staining of the timber gives a very good effect. It makes for very handsome tables.

Patterning on spalted beech

The Millennium table made from Boconnoc oak

I now very much enjoy our ancient trees, that is very old ones, and our veteran trees, that is those which are hanging on in the face of adversity.

We have welcomed the Ancient Tree Forum and their effervescent founder Ted Green to Boconnoc several times and I think they have done great work in promoting understanding of the value of trees in our environment.

Cornwall now has its own Ancient Tree Forum promoted by Cornwall County Council. →

The Ancient Tree Forum
Photo Min Wood

During its lifetime a tree provides a fascinating succession of habitats for other species.
We probably do not pay much attention to the bryophytes (mosses and liverworts) and the lichens on our trees but they do give the Cornish landscape a very special look in winter. The elegant tracery of the "fruticose" kinds, that is the straggly ones, can appear to turn a whole hillside grey. At Boconnoc we are fortunate to have one of the best sites in Western Europe for these long-lived organisms which is protected as a Site of Special Scientific Interest. Some ferns also make their home on the branches of trees.

Vegetation growing on a fallen tree

The cracks and crevices in the bark and the nooks and crannies made by the dieback of branches provide a haven for hundreds of species of invertebrates. Some feed from the tree, some such as the wood-)boring beetles and wasps make passages under the bark and some just hide away to avoid the attention of the birds which feed avidly on them if they have a chance. Some of the busiest of these are our native woodpeckers and it is for them in particular that we leave the standing trunks of dead trees here and there in the woodlands. Birds use the branches of trees to make nests safe from marauding mammals. One relationship between trees and a mammal has had devastating consequences for the regeneration of native trees. Would that we could poke out every drey of every grey squirrel.

In the park at Boconnoc, visitors may be surprised to see some trees which have ceased to produce leaves. They may be forgiven for describing them as being dead. In one sense they are. But where they are not likely to give rise to safety problems, we like to see some of them represented in the landscape. It is said that Humphry Repton would introduce such features in his new planting by importing "dead" trees. Not only are the skeletons of these trees a reminder of how we enjoyed them when they were in full leaf, the woody material continues to play its part in the ecosystem as I have described above. Is this "Art"? I think I will leave that for someone else to discuss.

It would not be realistic to allow trees to live out the whole of their lives in a small garden but wherever possible in parks, woodlands and public spaces we ought to respect our veteran trees and allow them to complete the full cycle from seed to final decay which is their natural place in our ecosystem. I believe that good land management should strike a balance between human needs and the needs of the environment in which we live; what some people call sustainable management. I want to see that there are trees planted and growing on at Boconnoc to become the ancient trees of the future. →

Skeleton tree

The mighty oak trees some 300 – 400 years old are gradually falling.

Log handler at timber yard

Cut trees stored for future processing

The trunks are taken from their original sites and stored for future processing. While in the past these would have been cut on the water powered sawmill into lintels, beams etc, regulation has limited its use and the mobile mill has replaced this historic machine. →

Log cutter and splitter

THE CORNISH GARDEN

One of the millponds showing outflow to leat

The old sawmill has a full system of two ponds and a leat leading downward through a large pipe to the turbine, which indirectly drives the saw.

An alternative use for this fine system is being considered, that is to generate electricity in place of driving the saw and putting power into the national grid. →

The leat leading to the turbine

The water-powered turbine below the sawmill

THE CORNISH GARDEN

Boconnoc Logs to Order
Telephone: 01208 872507 Fax: 01208 873836
Estate Office, Boconnoc, Lostwithiel, Cornwall, PL22 0RG

Beech trees continue to be blown over every winter.

It would be preferred to sell the large trunks for cut timber use but sadly the demand for this is almost nil. Limbs are removed and cut into 2 metre lengths to be collected by our forewarder for ongoing to stack in heaps for a year to dry before being turned into logs. The trunks are also removed to storage to be converted likewise. A thriving business within a 15 mile radius now exists giving customers an alternative to oil.

Cut logs ready for firewood

We have looked into converting the above into chips for central heating. The practicality of this lends itself to automatic feeding of central heating boilers. However, the energy required to reduce a solid timber to small pieces seems to outweigh this green and friendly concept along with the labour and fuel cost. "Chips", however, sold at the right price lend themselves well to garden use for controlling weed growth around plants and shrubs and act as a manure anyway.

The life cycle of trees either planted or grown simply by natural regeneration to old age continues as ever. Finding a balance between using the wood as a building product, a wood fuel or simply allowing it to rot away is vital to the future of woodland.

Boconnoc is open to groups by appointment and provides a wide range of wedding and hospitality facilities.
For further information visit the website at www.boconnocenterprises.co.uk .

For further information about ancient and veteran trees and Cornwall's Ancient Tree Forum visit www.cornwall.gov.uk/trees

GARDEN PHOTOGRAPHY
CHARLES FRANCIS

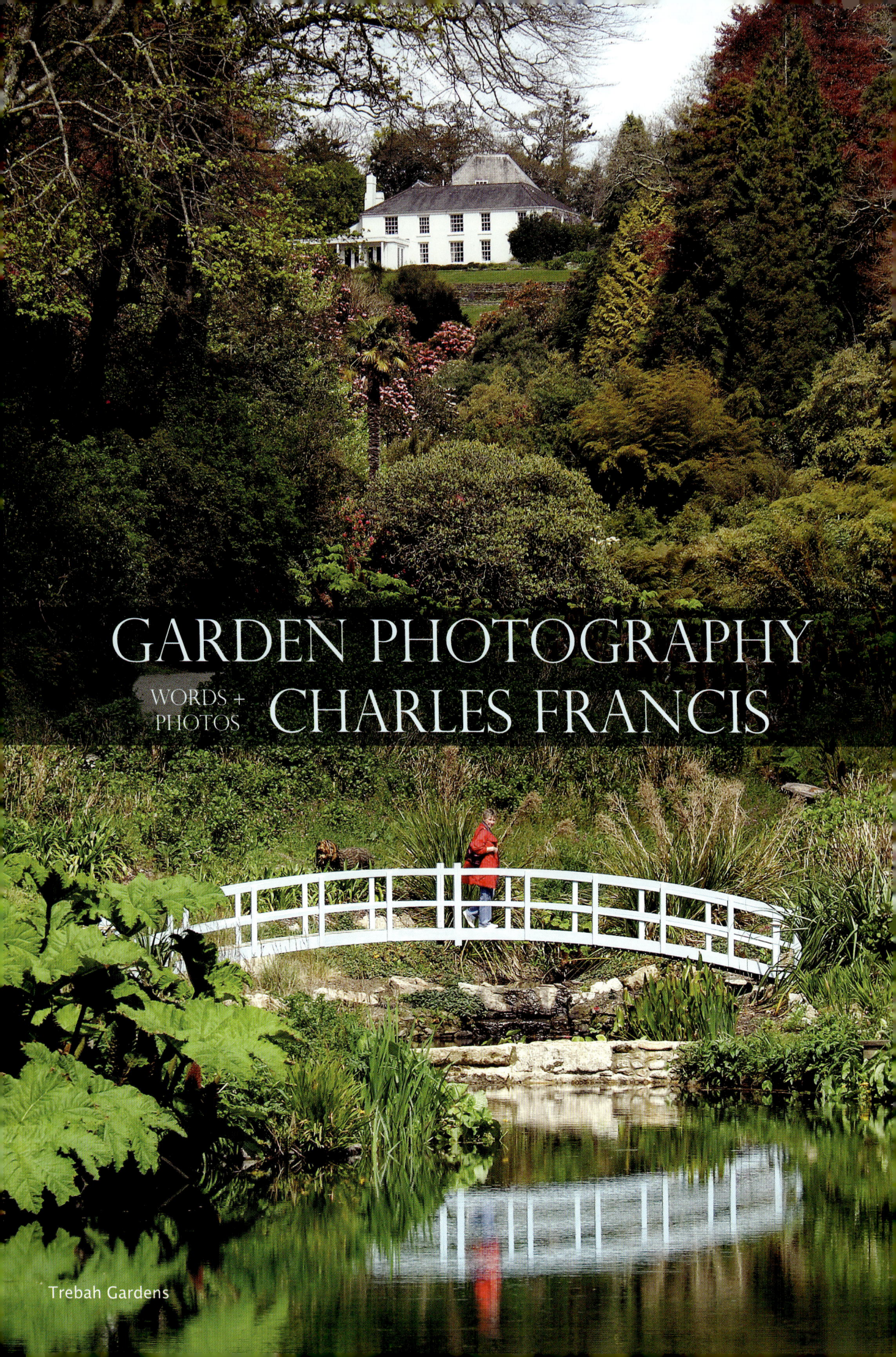

WORDS + PHOTOS

Trebah Gardens

Garden visiting on days-out and holidays is an activity which is sure to appeal to all keen gardeners.

Yet how often does one wish to record the day for future enjoyment only to find that the photos don't seem to quite do justice to the garden that one remembers in the mind?

On many occasions, a compact digital camera will be quite capable of producing a very satisfactory image and there is not the need to carry a massive camera bag, in fact the best camera in the world is of no use if it's at home in a cupboard, so a pocket-size one that can be carried all the time already has a definite advantage.

Setting-up the camera for your own needs is always necessary and read the handbook!

Digital photos can be recorded at different sizes and I would always recommend choosing the largest file size; although this gives fewer images on your memory card, it does mean that you can print them out at a later date if required. Smaller file sizes will be fine for viewing on a computer screen but that will be their limitation. On a long trip you can either take spare cards with you, or you can download onto a laptop / portable hard-drive, or burn them onto a CD so that you can format (delete) the card and continue shooting. Don't forget the battery charger if you are going to be away from home and maybe take a spare battery as well.

Usually the camera's automatic setting for "white balance" will be satisfactory but this can be altered and the "cloudy" setting will give a warmer image to cut out excessive blueness on dull days.

For natural-looking shots, it is best to avoid flash and this can usually be turned off, however, there is then a risk of camera shake, so it may be necessary to use a tripod or other support to steady it. If the purpose of the photo is purely for record rather than artisitic purposes, perhaps to remind you of a particular plant that you want to buy when you get back home, then flash is ideal on dull days as it will give a bright, clear, image.

Concentration on composition is undoubtedly one of the keys to successful pictures with any camera and looking carefully at the viewing screen or through the viewfinder to decide what will, or will not be, included is vital. Our vision tends to be quite selective and we can focus on an object and happily ignore its surroundings, but the camera sees all and records it, so make sure that you are not unwittingly including extraneous objects. Zooming in/out or moving in relation to your subject may achieve a better result.

Despite Cornwall being renowned for its good light for artists; for the photographer it can often be too dull/too bright or from the wrong angle.

HELIGAN
Fruit, Flowers and Herbs

Philip McMillan Browse

However, on those occasions when it is right, you just know that every photo is going to be a winner even as you press the shutter button; sadly such weather tends to be the exception rather than the rule!

In 1999, when I was recording the construction of the Eden Project we had rain on 100 consecutive days. A grey china-clay pit being filled with grey steel-work beneath a grey sky was pretty dispiriting and certainly not conducive to good postcard material!

Greater camera control is offered by digital single lens reflex cameras (DSLRs) which allow for more creativity. The foregoing remarks still apply but, in addition, their design permits more accurate visualisation of the final picture though the viewfinder as the depth of field can usually be checked and this shows how much of the picture will be in focus in front and behind the subject.

The picture above shows the way in which selective focus can concentrate the attention on a particular part of an image. This is achieved by using a large lens aperture, typically around f2.8, conversely, a small lens aperture of say f22 will allow the picture to have a greater depth of focus from foreground to background. →

The amount of light entering the camera is controlled not only by the lens aperture, but also by the shutter speed. This balancing act allows the quantity of light entering through the lens to be limited by the length of time that the shutter is open.

In the example above, the large lens aperture is offset by a high shutter speed, perhaps 1/1000th of a second. The same amount of light could enter the camera by having a wide aperture but this would necessitate a slower shutter speed of 1/15th of a second, there being a direct correlation between the two sets of numbers, as one is doubled the other is halved, thereby maintaining a constant.

Of course, the drawback of the slow shutter speed on outdoor photography is that there is a real risk of any slight breeze causing the plants to move, thus blurring the image. In a DSLR this can be reduced to an extent by altering the sensitivity (ISO) of the image sensor (in effect what was the film speed in pre-digital cameras). The higher the ISO speed, the faster shutter speed one can have for any given lens aperture. Nevertheless, as this can be changed between shots to suit the conditions, there is no longer the need to wait for the end of a film.

For those whose camera also has the option of recording RAW images, this retains all the information taken at the time, whereas if only Jpeg or Tiff information is saved the camera will have discarded details which it regards as superfluous. Although RAW files will use up more room on your memory card and in your computer, they work a bit like a time-machine in that you can subsequently return to your image and adjust the white balance for the lighting conditions and the exposure, as all this information is still available. Not necessary on all occasions by any means, but sometimes a very useful tool in the armoury.

Having got your pictures, you can either keep them as they are or you can make subsequent refinements using a computer editing program. Photoshop is the best known and a simplified version is sometimes included with the camera. Although some people used to regard enhancing an image as "cheating", it is now just another aspect of taking a photograph, the initial image merely being the negative from which one creates the final picture.

A good example of this is the way in which our eyes see the colour of some plants, sometimes they do not appear correctly on film as they reflect a colour which we do not see but which the camera's sensor picks up.

I recently photographed a tibouchina, which has a dark mauve flower, yet when it came up on the screen it had a pronounced blue shade, in this instance I was able to select the blue area in Photoshop and then adjust it to correct the colour. This picture also illustrates the way in which subsequent adjustments can be made to a RAW image by choosing the Cloudy white balance setting to compensate for the dull weather on the day it was taken.

Tibouchina at Lanterns

Colour is obviously all important in a picture and red is an example which stands out and will immediately draw the eye, so it has to be used carefully.

When I was commissioned to take the photograph of the Blue Bridge at Trebah Gardens (see previous page), I was asked to include a lady in a red coat on the bridge. Although I had intended to take a model along to pose for me, she was unavailable on the day, so I travelled hopefully, taking a red coat belonging to my wife, who was also unavailable on the day in question. When I arrived I scanned the car-park for a likely model but, as it was mid-week in early Spring, I saw only a group of probably retired people disembarking from a coach. Nevertheless, I was able to prevail on two or three of them to wear the coat and stand on the bridge whilst I took photos with a long lens from across the lower pool. In the end I got my photo of a lady in a red coat on the blue bridge and I think that she quite enjoyed it, despite the inevitable delays whilst other people crossed the bridge or the sun disappeared behind a cloud!

The same applies to people in a scene, our brains are designed to spot other humans at a glance.

Consequently, if you are going to have a person in your picture, make sure that they are going to benefit the final composition, as opposite. Usually, garden visitors tend to keep moving so, if someone is in the way, wait a little while until they have moved out of shot. Try hiding the figure in both of these photos and you will immediately see the difference that it makes.

Caerhays Castle

www.alison-hodge.co.uk

sculpture by Carole Vincent

Alison Hodge Publishers

Heathers of The Lizard

David McClintock

Illustrated by Marjorie Blamey

The definitive guide to the heathers of The Lizard peninsula by the former president of the Heather Society with superb colour illustrations by wildflower artist Marjorie Blamey

Price £1.50 (plus 50p p&p) available from:
Pat Ward, Membership Secretary, Poltisko, Silver Hill, Perranwell Station, Truro TR3 7LP

Pentewan Valley Nurseries

Friendly family run business with vast assortment of perennials, shrubs, conifers, fruit & ornamental trees, herbs, cordylines, climbers, roses & fuschias etc.

Compost, seeds, pot plants & gift ideas now in stock. Bedding plants. Ready planted pots, baskets in season & much, much more.

Pentewan Road, St Austell
on B3273 to Mevagissey.
Tel/Fax : 01726 842360

Cornish Cut Flowers

I am compiling a directory of Cornish flower growers, large and small, at the moment. Most cut flowers are being brought in from abroad, a practice that in terms of climate change and supporting Cornish growers, is not sustainable (at present rates).

If you are a cut flower grower, or know of someone who is, please let me know. People are asking for local flowers more and more. Thank you for your help.

Mrs Jo Willis Fleming T: 01726 842412 E: galowras.mill@virgin.net

Mally Francis
Botanical Painting Courses

Regular weekly classes in a large well-lit and fully-equipped studio at Heligan.

Ideal for beginners or experienced artists

www.thewagonhouse.com

"Tranquil, absorbing and very informative"

For further details please contact:
Mally Francis
The Wagon House,
Heligan Manor,
St Ewe,
Cornwall PL26 6EW
Tel 01726 844505

From the ends of the Earth by Christian Lamb

An eclectic and highly readable mix of gardening, history and autobiography; a book as original as her garden.

Over 140 illustrations & photographs. 210 pages packed with accounts of the intrepid and enterprising pioneers who brought back new and exotic plants from the ends of the earth.

Price £17.99

*For further details and ordering information
please visit www.christianlamb.co.uk*

To advertise in the 2009 CGS Journal, please contact Charles Francis 01726 844505 or email thewagonhouse@mac.com for details

ONCE VISITED,
IMPOSSIBLE TO FORGET...

TREWITHEN

There is nowhere quite like Trewithen.

With its magnificent collection of camellias, rhododendrons and magnolias, its wonderful woodland walks and heritage family home, Trewithen is a rare and unique Cornish gem.

OPENING TIMES
Gardens: 1 Mar-30 Sept. Mon-Sat (Sun Mar-May). 10am-4pm
Nurseries: All year. Mon-Sat. 9am-4.30pm
House: 1 Apr-31 July. Mon-Tues. 2pm-4pm

TREWITHEN GARDENS & NURSERIES
Grampound, Nr Truro, Cornwall TR2 4DD
Tel: 01726 883647
Web: www.trewithengardens.co.uk

Trebah

WINNER
Popular Restaurant / Cafe
of the Year
Cornwall Tourism Awards 2006

The exotic and friendly garden by the sea

- Open daily 10.30am to 5pm (last admission)
- Free to NT and RHS members 1st Nov to 29th Feb
- Dogs are most welcome, on leads
- For seasonal events and special promotions visit our website
- Trebah's award-winning Planters Cafe offers home cooked dishes using fresh Cornish produce
- Stylish gifts at the Gallery and Garden Shops

OPEN EVERY DAY OF THE YEAR
www.trebah-garden.co.uk   Mawnan Smith, near Falmouth   01326 252200

Tree Ferns in Cornwall

A brief history by Cindy Clench

Jungle Supervisor
The Lost Gardens of Heligan

Photo Charles Francis

Tree Ferns are an Australian species, *Dicksonia antarctica*, named in honour of James Dickson, a founder member of the London Horticultural Society.

It is a slow-growing species, which in its native habitat can develop a trunk up to 40 feet tall, with fronds up to 13 feet long. A new crop of fronds develops each Spring from the top of the trunk, and the old fronds slowly die off, hanging down to form a skirt around the gradually rising trunk - eventually rotting off.

The new fronds, with their delicate fiddleback appearance as they unfold, are also a delight. It is difficult to determine the age of a Tree Fern as it has no annual rings or other indicators. Technically the trunk is a rhizome with adventitious roots, whose main purpose is to stabilise the plant.

Various stories have been told about how these Tree Ferns arrived in Cornwall - some (in the latter half of the nineteenth century) were possibly used as ballast in ships returning from Australia. However, the majority of the Tree Ferns which abound in Cornwall and are certainly of pre-Great War vintage, derived from the efforts of John Garland Treseder, who had emigrated from Truro to Australia in the 1870s and established a nursery at Paramatta in New South Wales. Over some two decades from 1892 onwards, he sent literally hundreds of dry trunks directly to various estate owners in Cornwall, and latterly to the re-established Treseder Nursery at Moresk. These importations continued up until 1914. The trunks arrived, by ship, at Falmouth and (so legend has it) were off-loaded on to railway trucks, which transported them to Truro and then along the viaduct to just above Moresk, where they were heaved over the parapet and dropped into the stream that ran beside the nursery. Here they remained until they had soaked up enough water to rehydrate and begin the process of expanding new fronds during the next Spring. In the early years of the twentieth century they were a regular item in the Treseder catalogues.

There are fossils of the earliest *Dicksonia antarctica* which date back to the Jurassic period, making this a truly prehistoric plant. Looking at them today, with their massive, moss-covered trunks, it is easy to be transported back in time.

Cover story: Dicksonia antarctica

Extracted from *Dicksonia antarctica*, an article by Cindy Clench from the book "Heligan Survivors".

Inspired and edited by Philip McMillan Browse. Published by Alison Hodge. Spring 2007

**Available from:
The Lost Gardens of Heligan
Pentewan, St Austell, Cornwall PL26 6EN
Tel 01726 845100
www.heligan.com**

Photographed by Charles Francis in the Lost Gardens of Heligan